Kidlicious

Fun & Healthy Recipes That Kids Love!

by

Stephanie & Anneliese Howard

D1411350

Go to **www.kidlicious.com** for more tips and to watch videos of some of our favorite recipes being made!

ISBN: 978-0-9835594-1-2
Cover and interior design by: Douglas Taylor
Edited by: Helene Thomas
Photographs by: Acorn Studios
Illustrations by: Eric Pletcher

Acknowledgments.

Many have said that it takes a village to raise a child. But what you may not know is that it also takes a village to write a cookbook. Many talented people helped make Kidlicious the exciting health resource that it is. I would like to give special thanks to all of those who helped me through the process.

Evelyn Kissinger, a registered dietitian and lifestyle educator, inspired me with her enthusiastic health talks for children and offered advice to help insure that our mystery in the classroom series had accurate information. Another good friend, Kristin Collins, offered her expertise, as is a pediatric Dietitian. She counsels with young children on a regular basis and knows what they most need to hear, and how they can best understand the information presented.

A licensed counselor, Rhonda Hill helped to track down the information we used in our "for Parent's Only" sections to help us build better families.

In many respects the real experts are the moms who are daily working with their children, feeding them the best foods and teaching them the important lessons of life. I want to give a big thank you to all of the moms who consulted, offered suggestions, and tested recipes.

Amie Hubbard, mother of 5

Lori Randall, mother of 2

Amy Austin, mother of 3

Emilee DeVasher, mother of 2

Eileen Iwankiw , mother of 2

Midori Sliger, mother of 1

Andrea Moody, mother of 3

Monica Flower, mother of 3

Annette Metz, mother of 2

Beth Thomas, mother of 2

Tami LeRoux, mother of 3

Without the tireless efforts of Amie Hubbard, Lori Randall and Sarah Frain the beautiful photographs in this book would not be possible.

Last but by no means least, a huge thanks to all of the teachers and students at Gobles Junior Academy who were eager taste testers during hot lunches. Many of them appear on the pages if this book, helping to cook up some Kidliciousness.

Contents

Saddle up your taste buds...
we are headed for an
ADVENTURE!

Have you ever been on an adventure? I have an uncle John, who is known for taking us all on crazy adventures I will never forget all the fun we had roaming through the dark woods and climbing up steep mountains. We even made it to an island once! Sometimes those adventures seemed too hard when we were climbing a steep hill or being attacked by mosquitoes. But at the end of the day, when we were home and resting, it was the BEST adventure ever! There is nothing like the feeling of a completed adventure. I felt great because I tried something new and didn't give up!

"One time Mom came home with a Durian. I was excited to try this new exotic fruit."

Uncle John's adventures are fun, but my mom and I like to go on a different kind of adventure. We go on KITCHEN adventures! It is so fun to search out and taste new foods; to create new recipes no one has ever tried before. Our favorite thing to do is to take regular recipes and turn them into healthy plant-based meals that our bodies can use better. They don't always come out right (just ask Daddy!) But we keep working until it passes the KIDLICIOUS test... healthy AND delicious!

Sometimes food adventures can be hard too! One time Mom came home with a Durian. I was excited to try this new exotic fruit. It looked like a big porcupine! But when we cut it open, ugh, it smelled like rotten onions and dirty gym socks. I wondered, "Do people actually eat this stuff?!" With a little detective work we learned that it was a popular fruit in Malaysia. How could that be?! Then we got to thinking. People must like the food they eat the most. After all isn't that why people from India like Indian food, and Chinese people like Chinese food?

People grow up learning to like the foods that are available around them, so the foods we eat most tend to be our favorites. If we eat healthy plant-based foods most of the time, our taste buds will adjust. Then these new healthy foods can become our favorites.

My mom doesn't let me say I don't like a food. She just says that I am learning to like it. She read somewhere that you need to try a new food 10-15 times before you'll really like it, so even if I think I don't like something, I try it again anyway. I just might like it now!

So, if you are ready, saddle up your taste buds, you are about to go on an amazing food adventure!

Parents, Don't Miss This....

Using the Book

Adventures are no fun when you're all alone. We designed this book with family in mind. Working together in the kitchen is a great way to bond, and to have fun. The experts have proven that the family that cooks together and eats together tends to be healthier and happier. (See page 160 for more information.)

Cooking can be even more fun and rewarding when you share your creations with others! We have included some fun ways to package your food to give as gifts. Food gifts are a great way to say thank you to everyone from teachers to the mailman, and from the Librarian to the guy who picks up your trash. Plus, it will help the whole family think of ways they can bless others.

There is an old adage that says: "Too little to save, too much to dump. That's what makes mommies plump!" How true it is that moms, and sometimes dads end up eating more food than they intended because there is just a little left and they hate to see it go to waste. Those little bits of food can add up to lots of added pounds in the course of a year. If you watch the lunch box tips closely you will learn how to turn little bits of leftovers into prize winning lunches that will save your waistline and your wallet.

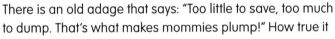

Introduction...

Anneliese and her friends at school love to figure out why things happen and how things work. When they see something they don't understand, they just have to find out how and why it happened. You can help them find the answers to some mysteries. At the beginning of each chapter there's a mystery to be solved. Be on the lookout for the clues hidden in the chapter, so you can solve the mystery!

CASE #1:

Mystery of the Good Grades

Case Notes:

Beth used to get bad grades in school. Recently she started doing a lot better. She even got an A on a math test. WOW! How did she do it? Let's examine the evidence and see what happened!

Interview Transcript:

Investigator: So, Beth, what changes have you made recently?

Beth: Well, nothing really… except… I used to sleep in too late and miss breakfast. But Mom got a great new recipe for Refrigerator Oatmeal (Page 21)! It is so quick and easy that breakfast is ready in no time and I never have to miss it!

Investigator: Anything else?

Beth: I can't think of anything. I sure do feel a lot better now. I can concentrate on my work and I LOVE getting good grades! I even have more energy to play!

Evidence:

- Beth's grades have improved dramatically.

- She eats breakfast.

- She has a lot of energy.

Watch for the blue magnifying glass to find clues throughout the chapter!

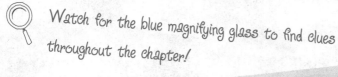

THE VERDICT

Getting enough sleep and eating breakfast have made a big difference for Beth. They help her act nicer, and gets better grades in school.

We know that kids who eat a healthy breakfast get better grades and are more attentive in class. They also have more energy and less behavior problems.

Use left over oatmeal to make
Oatmeal Bread (page 141)

GLUTEN FREE!

Breakfast Banana Split

Would you rather have a banana split for breakfast instead of oatmeal? But Mom would never go for that! Unless... What if you made your oatmeal into a banana split?!! Now I think you've got something!

INGREDIENTS

4 bananas

4 cups cooked oatmeal (make it very thick so you can scoop it with an ice cream scoop)

½ cup crushed pineapple

1 pound strawberries, mashed

1 recipe Hot Fudge Sauce (page 123)

1 recipe Whipped Topping (page 123)

½ cup chopped peanuts

4 sweet cherries (optional)

DIRECTIONS

1. Cut banana in half lengthwise and place in ice cream dish or bowl.

2. Using an ice cream scoop, place 3 scoops of oatmeal on each split banana.

3. Top one scoop with pineapple, one with strawberries, and one with carob fudge sauce.

4. Add a dollop of whipped topping and sprinkle with nuts.

5. Put a cherry on top and enjoy!

LUNCH BOX: The left over fruit makes a yummy fruit salad to carry in your lunch. Don't forget to add a little dollop of the whipped topping!

Try This!

Oatmeal Sundae (one scoop version), just slice the banana in a bowl, add a scoop of oatmeal, and top with whatever toppings you like.

GLUTEN FREE when you use gluten free oats or other gluten free hot cereal.

Beth always chooses whole grain cereals and breads at breakfast with lots of vitamins and minerals that help her body work better.

Smiling Pancakes

Smiles are contagious...so start your day off right with Smiling Pancakes! They will keep you smiling all day!

INGREDIENTS

Dry Ingredients:

1½ cups whole wheat pastry flour (or 1 cup whole wheat flour and ½ cup unbleached white flour)

½ cup unbleached white flour

½ cup cornmeal

1 tablespoon aluminum-free baking powder

2 tablespoons cane juice crystals, or sugar

½ teaspoon salt

Wet Ingredients:

2 cups non-dairy milk

¼ cup oil

Make this into a mix (page 10) for a quick breakfast so you can have pancakes more often.

DIRECTIONS

1. Preheat griddle pan to about 350°.

2. Mix dry ingredients together in a medium sized bowl.

3. Pour wet ingredients into the dry ingredients and use a whisk to mix well (a whisk helps get out the lumps).

4. See the next page for how to make the different faces, but for regular pancakes use a ¹/₃ cup measuring cup to carefully pour the batter onto the hot griddle.

5. When the batter starts to bubble on top and the edges look dry, flip over the pancake and cook until golden.

6. Remove pancakes from griddle and place on a plate. You can cover the plate with a large bowl to keep them warm while you cook the rest.

Watch how it's done on **www.kidlicious.com**

QUICK: Clean out an old ketchup bottle and use it to squeeze just the right amount of batter onto your hot griddle...no drips.

Smiley Gift

Share your smiles with style! Go to **www.kidlicious.com** to watch an easy video about how to wrap up this pancake mix to share with someone who needs a smile.

Pancake Mix

INGREDIENTS

4 ½ cups whole wheat pastry flour

1 ½ cups unbleached white flour

1 ½ cups cornmeal

⅓ cup non-dairy milk powder

⅓ cup cane juice crystals

3 tablespoons aluminum-free baking powder

½ tablespoon salt

DIRECTIONS

1 Mix all ingredients in a large airtight container.

2 To make pancakes, add 2 ½ cups of mix to 2 cups water and ¼ cup oil. Mix well.

3 Using a ^{z} cup measure, pour onto a hot griddle. When the batter starts to bubble on top and the edges look dry, flip over the pancake and cook until golden.

4 Flip over and cook the other side until golden.

Make a Monkey for Breakfast:

1. Put ⅓ cup of the batter in a separate bowl.

2. Add 1 tablespoon carob powder or cocoa powder (for a darker pancake).

3. Use the darker batter to make a larger pancake for the monkey head.

4. Using the lighter batter make two smaller pancakes for his ears and one a little large for the mouth and nose part of his face.

5. Use some carob chips or chocolate chips for his eyes, nose, and mouth.

Have a Piggy Pancake:

1. Make pancake using ⅓ cup of batter and 2 small pancakes using ⅛ cup (2 tablespoons) each.

2. Place a large pancake on your plate.

3. Use the handle of a wooden spoon to poke 2 holes in one of the small pancakes for the nostrils of your piggy's snout.

4. Place your "snout" in center of the large pancake.

5. Cut the other small pancake in half for ears.

6. Use blueberries for eyes.

Beary Special Pancakes:

1. Make one large pancake using ⅓ cup of batter and three small ones using about ⅛zw of a cup (2 tablespoons) each.

2. Place the large pancake in the center of the plate.

3. Add two of the small pancakes for ears.

4. Use the last pancake for his nose.

5. Place 3 raisins for the eyes and nose. We used scissors to cut the mouth from one of our homemade Fruit Rollups (page 33).

Big Nose Pancakes:

1. Make one large pancake.

2. Slice a strawberry lengthwise for eyes and then add two blueberries for the pupils.

3. Cut off the end of the banana for the nose. You can make his nose as big as you like!

4. Use a slice of apple, peach, or orange for the mouth.

How do you eat your waffle?

Beth really enjoys eating nuts for breakfast to give her brain and body a boost.

Gluten Free Power Waffles

Sometimes we have waffles for breakfast. Sometimes, for a special supper on a Saturday night, my mom makes Frozen Fruit Ice Cream (page 129) to go on top of the waffles! Don't I have the best mom ever?!

INGREDIENTS

3 cups rolled oats

½ cup cornmeal

½ cup garbanzo flour

4 cups water

2 tablespoons honey or agave nectar

2 tablespoons oil

1 tablespoon vanilla or maple flavoring

1 teaspoon salt

DIRECTIONS

1. Turn on the waffle iron to preheat. Turn oven on to the warm setting to keep baked waffles warm while making the remaining waffles.

2. Stir all ingredients together in a bowl.

3. Blend the batter in a blender or with a stick blender. It is okay if it is still a little chunky.

4. Spray waffle iron with non-stick cooking spray.

5. Pour batter onto hot waffle iron. Close lid and bake 10-12 minutes.

6. Place waffles on rack in warm oven to keep warm and crisp while the other waffles cook or cool on a cooling rack before freezing or stacking.

LUNCH BOX: Make a terrific gluten free sandwich by using a waffle instead of bread! To keep the waffle from getting soggy, pack everything separate and put it all together at school.

Put left over waffles in the freezer for a quick breakfast. Reheat by placing in a warm oven or toaster oven for a few minutes while you are getting dressed.

Beth is smart. She gets breakfast ready the night before so there is plenty of time to enjoy breakfast. That Refrigerator Oatmeal recipe (page 21) is her favorite.

Strawberry Shortcake

My birthday is in June, and strawberry season is in June! I don't think it should be a surprise that I would want strawberry shortcake for my birthday breakfast. See if you can talk your mom into going to a U-pick farm. Picking your own berries is so much fun!

INGREDIENTS

1 recipe Shortcake Biscuits

2 pounds fresh strawberries, sliced or diced

Non-dairy milk - vanilla is nice.

Shortcake Biscuits

Dry Ingredients:

3 cups whole wheat pastry flour (barley flour works great for wheat free)

3 tablespoons cane juice crystals or sugar

1 tablespoon aluminum-free baking powder

¼ teaspoon salt

Wet Ingredients:

1 cup non-dairy milk, unsweetened

⅓ cup oil

DIRECTIONS

1. Crumble a biscuit or two into each bowl.

2. Pile on the strawberries.

3. Pour non-dairy milk over the berries.

4. Eat immediately.

Shortcake Biscuits

1. Preheat oven to 375°. Coat muffin tins with non-stick cooking spray.

2. Mix dry ingredients together in a medium sized bowl.

3. Add wet ingredients to dry ingredients, mix together just until you don't see dry flour anymore. Be careful not to over mix.

4. If batter seems too thick, add more milk, 1 tablespoon at a time. These are drop biscuits so they should scoop and drop easily from a spoon.

5. Fill prepared muffin tins with batter; bake 15-18 minutes, or until light brown.

Strawberry Shortcake Gift Basket

Did a neighbor move in next door? They may not have their kitchen unpacked yet! Why not take over a strawberry shortcake gift basket? Go to www.kidlicious.com to watch an easy "how to" video.

Breakfast Pizza

You will never want to skip breakfast when pizza is being served! The tofu and cheese are amazing together, and it even smiles back at you! You can't get a better breakfast than that!

INGREDIENTS

6 whole grain English muffins

⅓ cup Real Tomato Ketchup (page 139) or pizza sauce

1 recipe Scrambled Tofu

1 package non-dairy cheese, slices or shredded (I like Galaxy brand)

6 black olives, sliced (for eyes)

12 slices red pepper (for mouth)

DIRECTIONS

1. Split English muffins in half and place on cookie sheet.

2. Spread 1 tablespoon of Real Tomato Ketchup on each English muffin.

3. Top with a layer of scrambled tofu and a little non dairy cheese.

4. Use olives and peppers to make a face.

5. Bake at 350 for 10 -12 minutes.

Scrambled Tofu

We use this in on our *Breakfast Pizza*, but it's also delicious on its own, or even in a sandwich for lunch!

INGREDIENTS

2 packages (14 ounces) water-packed tofu, extra firm, well drained

1 tablespoon oil

1 small onion, diced small (optional)

½ small green or red bell pepper, diced small (optional)

¼ cup nutritional yeast flakes

3 tablespoons chicken style seasoning

1½ teaspoons garlic powder

1 teaspoon onion powder

1 teaspoon salt

¼ teaspoon turmeric (optional, for color)

½ cup vegetarian sausage crumbles or **4** vegetarian sausage links crumbled (optional)

DIRECTIONS

1. Drain excess water from tofu by pressing it between some clean dishtowels or placing it in a colander with something heavy on top of it for about 10 minutes.

2. Heat oil in a large skillet over medium heat. Add onions and bell pepper and cook 2-3 minutes.

3. Crumble tofu into pan with your fingers or use a spatula to break it into pieces.

4. Add remaining ingredients to the skillet; cook until tofu is lightly browned and slightly dry, stirring occasionally. This could take from 10 to 20 minutes, depending on the tofu. The longer the tofu is cooked, the firmer it will be.

LUNCH BOX: Make a Breakfast for Lunch Burrito (page 59) with the leftovers for an excellent breakfast for lunch.

One thing Beth really enjoys eating at breakfast is nuts. She especially likes walnuts in her cereal. Sometimes she uses almond butter to give her body and brain the healthy fats that she needs to think well and play without getting tired.

Fruit Pizza

Pizza! Pizza! This is the second pizza we have for breakfast, but this one is sweeeeeet! YUM!

Very Berry Fruit Pizza

½ cup soy cream cheese

2-3 tablespoons all fruit berry jelly (strawberry, blueberry or raspberry)

4 whole grain English muffins

sliced strawberries

coconut (optional)

Peaches & Cream Fruit Pizza

½ cup soy cream cheese

2-3 tablespoons all fruit peach or apricot jelly

4 whole grain English muffins

1 peach thinly sliced

coconut (optional)

DIRECTIONS

1. Mix soy cream cheese and jelly in a small bowl until combined.

2. Split the English muffins and spread 1 tablespoon of cream on each half.

3. Decorate with fresh fruit and coconut.

LUNCH BOX: This is a great way to have breakfast for lunch! Just pack your cream cheese and jelly mixture in a small container and spread it on at lunchtime.

Beth eats at least 2 fruits at breakfast, fresh fruits are best but sometimes she eats frozen, canned or dried fruits when it is not fruit season.

Flavor combos to try...

➡ **Blueberry Peach**
Use peach yogurt and fresh or frozen Blueberries.

➡ **Cherry Vanilla**
Use Vanilla yogurt, sweet cherries, and a few toasted pecans.

➡ **Mixed berry**
Use any berry yogurt and fresh berries.

➡ **Mango Strawberry**
Use strawberry yogurt and fresh or frozen mangos.

➡ **Raspberry Peach**
Use raspberry yogurt with peaches and raspberries.

➡ **Mandarin Orange**
Use vanilla yogurt and fresh or canned mandarin oranges.

➡ **Apple Cranberry**
Use vanilla yogurt, diced apple, and a few dried cranberries.

Refrigerator Oatmeal

THE perfect "school day" breakfast! It can be made 2 or 3 days in advance, and it is a meal in itself. You don't even have to set the table – just a spoon and a jar of yumminess! (or should I say Kidliciousness?)

INGREDIENTS

¼ cup uncooked old fashioned rolled oats

⅓ cup soy, almond or coconut yogurt

¼ cup non-dairy milk

¼ cup fruit, fresh or frozen (mango, peach, apple, strawberries)

1 teaspoon dried chia seeds

1 tablespoon dried fruit or nuts (optional)

Pinch salt

DIRECTIONS

1. Toast oats in a 300° oven for 10 - 15 minutes stirring occasionally.

2. Place all ingredients in a half pint jar or container with a lid.

3. Shake well to mix everything up and place in refrigerator overnight.

4. Eat it cold right out of the fridge or warm slightly in the microwave.

LUNCH BOX: If you like to have breakfast for lunch, these pack easily in your lunch.

GLUTEN FREE when you use gluten free oats.

For an extra burst of flavor and sweetness add a teaspoon of all fruit or low sugar jelly to the mix.

The Greatest Thing Since Sliced Bread

Cereal for breakfast AGAIN! No worries! Just have something different on your toast for some fun. You can use whole grain bread, whole grain English muffins or even whole grain bagels to make things interesting.

You can make your ordinary old peanut butter toast more fun with a few slices of banana and raisins.

Just a few slices of avocado on a whole grain English muffin and a sprinkle of salt make a great breakfast.

Beth likes to be in bed early at night so she can pop out of bed in the morning feeling good and ready for a healthy breakfast!

Here is one I bet you've never had! Non-dairy margarine, nutritional yeast flakes, and just a sprinkle of salt. It is loaded with B vitamins, which we like to call happy vitamins, because B vitamins can help make you happy!

You can even make it into a little flag if you're feeling patriotic! Just spread toast with soy cream cheese. Fill one corner with blueberries for stars, and then spread a little all fruit strawberry preserves over the rest. Use Banana slices for white stripes.

MYSTERY IN THE CLASSROOM

CASE #2:

How Frank won the Award

Case Notes: Last year, Frank was sick almost every month. This year he hasn't missed any school at all. In fact, he got the citizenship award for the first time! What made the difference for Frank? What helped him to stay healthier? Let's solve the mystery!

Interview Transcript:

 Watch for clues!

Investigator: Frank, what do you think has helped you stay healthier this year?

Frank: Last summer I went to a kids' healthy cooking program and learned a lot about how to stay healthy. One thing I learned was that fruits and vegetables have phytochemicals (FIGHT-O-Chemicals), and those phytochemicals help fight off germs that can make me sick.

Investigator: Really?! That is interesting! What else did you learn?

Frank: I learned that phytochemicals are in colorful foods….each color has special phytochemicals….it's like eating a rainbow of colors. The more different colors I eat, the more different phytochemicals I get. Each phytochemical is a different color and each one helps a different part of my body to stay healthy. I can eat a whole rainbow of colors every day to be healthy all over!

Investigator: That sounds like a great class! I wish I could have gone too!

Evidence:
- Frank has missed a lot less school this year than he did last year.
- Frank started eating 5-8 servings of colorful fruits and vegetables every day.

THE VERDICT

Eating 5-8 servings of fruits and vegetables of all different colors helped Frank stay healthy and fight off germs! You need to eat a rainbow of colors every day to help you stay strong and healthy!

Eating Rainbows!

FUN FRUIT SALADS

Fruit is always tasty, but it's more fun to eat when it's cute!

Sweet Butterflies

INGREDIENTS: Oranges, sliced Grapes

1. Cut orange slices into fourths (four equal pieces)

2. Arrange grapes on plate in lines of 3

3. Add orange wings

Melon Kebabs

INGREDIENTS: Cantaloupe, cut into 1-inch thick slices, honeydew melon, cut into 1-inch thick slices, watermelon, cut into 1-inch thick slices

1. Use a small cookie cutter to make shapes out of the fruit slices.

2. Slide each piece of fruit onto a skewer or popsicle stick.

Use the scraps in Frosty Fruit (page 127)

Tropical Paradise

INGREDIENTS: Banana, Kiwi, Mandarin oranges, or pineapple chunks

1. Slice a banana in half lengthwise and place it on the plate.

2. Cut slices and "bend" banana slices to look like a palm tree.

3. Peel and slice Kiwi and arrange them in slices to look like palm tree fronds.

4. Place oranges or pineapple at the bottom to look like sand.

Mango Hedgehog

INGREDIENTS: 1 mango, 4 raisins, 2 red berries

1. Because of the big pit in the middle of a mango you can't cut down the center. Move your knife over to the right just a little and make a cut.

2. Do the same on the other side.

3. With a small paring knife, cut the fruit from each half into small cubes without cutting through the skin!

4. Using your thumbs, press the mango inside out. Mango hedgehog! Add raisins for eyes and a small berry for the nose.

5. To eat, simply pick him up and bite off the pieces. Or you can use a knife and let the pieces fall into a bowl.

The Racecar

INGREDIENTS: 1 banana, peeled, 1 kiwi sliced, 1 strawberry stemmed, 1 blueberry, 3 toothpicks

1. Place toothpicks through banana where the wheels should be.

2. Add kiwi slices to make wheels.

3. Add one more toothpick for the driver. Use the strawberry for the body and the blueberry for the head.

Berry Flower Garden

INGREDIENTS: Honeydew Melon, Large Strawberries, Raspberries, Red and yellow Toothpicks

1. Dice up honeydew melon and place in small bowl.

2. Slice strawberries into circles. Using a small flower shaped cutter, cut them into flowers.

3. Place strawberry flowers onto toothpicks and arrange in melon.

4. Put Raspberries on toothpicks to look like tulips and arrange in melon.

LUNCH BOX: Instead of Nachos make it a dip. Put Peanut Butter Drizzle and Hot Fudge Sauce in small containers for you to dip apple slices in.

Red, Orange, Yellow, Green, Blue and Purple, Frank eats a whole rainbow everyday to make sure he has all of those Fight-O-Chemicals!

Apple Nachos

Sweeeeet Nachos. This is way better than the way everybody else does nachos!

INGREDIENTS

¼ cup sliced almonds

¼ cup pecans

3 crispy apples

¼ cup lemon or orange juice

3 tablespoons Peanut Butter Drizzle (see below)

3 tablespoons Hot Fudge Sauce (page 123)

¼ cup dates or raisins

Peanut Butter Drizzle

1 tablespoon peanut butter

1 tablespoon maple syrup or agave nectar

DIRECTIONS

1. Place almonds and pecans on a cookie sheet. Put in a 200° oven for about 5-8 minutes, until they start to smell really good and turn a little brown.

2. Slice apples very thin, place in a bowl and pour juice over the apples, mix together. (This keeps them from turning brown.)

3. Warm the Peanut Butter Drizzle and the Hot Fudge Sauce in the microwave for 10 - 20 seconds until they are a little runny (the time will depend on your microwave).

4. Remove apples from juice and dry slightly with paper towel.

5. Spread apples over platter or large plate, like you would do with chips for nachos.

6. Drizzle with the Peanut Butter Drizzle and Hot Fudge Sauce.

7. Sprinkle with raisins or dates, almonds and pecans.

8. Serve with lots of napkins.

Peanut Butter Drizzle

Mix peanut butter and maple syrup in a small bowl and warm in the microwave for about 10 seconds.

Toast nuts in the microwave by placing nuts on a glass plate in a single layer. Cook in microwave on high for about 5 minutes stirring every minute or so.

Nacho Ordinary Neighbors

It's fun to get to know all of your neighbors! This is a good way to let your neighbors know that you and your family are something special. www.kidlicious.com.

LUNCH BOX: Instead of making fresh applesauce every week, you can freeze applesauce in individual size cups so they will be ready for your lunch when you need them. You don't even have to thaw them first.

Try This!
Add 2-3 tablespoons of Berry Sauce (page 35) to 1 cup of unsweetened applesauce. Now you have berry applesauce.

Happy Sauce

GLUTEN FREE!

My cousin calls applesauce "happy sauce" because applesauce makes him happy. This homemade version is more like supercalifragilistic sauce because it makes you extra happy. I love it on my pancakes or waffles and it is a perfect way to add another color to your lunchbox. We have 3 flavors for you to try.

Applesauce

6 sweet apples, like Macintosh or Yellow Delicious (using 2 or 3 different kids of apples makes it taste even better)

½ cup water or apple juice

Harvest Peach Applesauce

3 sweet apples

3 ripe peaches

½ cup water or apple juice

Plumb Good Applesauce

3 sweet apples

4-5 ripe plumbs

½ cup water or apple juice

DIRECTIONS

1. Wash the fruit very well with a vegetable wash to remove any germs or pesticides that may be on the fruit.

2. Use an apple corer slicer to cut the apples. Cut the peaches or plumbs into wedges. Don't worry about peeling.

3. Place the fruit in a large saucepan and add the water or juice.

4. Bring the mixture to a boil, reduce heat to medium-low. Cover the pot and cook for 15-20 minutes or until the fruit is soft. Stir occasionally so it doesn't burn. If your pan gets dry just add a little more water or juice.

5. Remove the mixture from the heat and allow to cool a little.

6. Pour cooked fruit into the blender or food processor and blend until smooth. For chunky applesauce simply mash with a potato masher.

An Apple A Day Gift

An apple a day keeps the doctor away, right? Just for fun, why don't you take a few jars of your homemade applesauce to share with the doctors and nurses at your next appointment? www.kidlicious.com.

The darker the color the more powerful the vitamins and phytochemicals! Frank loves dark green veggies

LUNCH BOX: Fruit Roll-ups made with real fruit are a sweet addition to your lunch.

Rainbow Fruit Roll-Ups

I can't pack enough of these in my lunch box. All my friends beg me to share. Of course, I always do. We all think that this is a super fun way to eat a rainbow of colors...it seems like candy, but it is really yummy fruit.

INGREDIENTS

4 cups fruit (berries, peaches, mango, kiwi, etc.)

¼ cup dried fruit* (optional for sweetness). Dried pineapple works well because it does not have a strong flavor. It goes with almost anything.

. . . .

* Look for "low-sugar" dried fruit.

If you spread your fruit too thick you may find that it takes a lot longer, but that's okay. It will be very yummy in the end.

DIRECTIONS

1. Preheat oven to the lowest setting 170-200°, and line a cookie sheet with parchment paper.

2. Place all ingredients in a saucepan, mash slightly with a potato masher.

3. Cook on medium heat for about 20 minutes until the fruit is very soft and about half of the liquid boils away and it starts to get thick.

4. Allow to cool and pour into a blender and blend until smooth.

5. Spread the puree over the parchment lined cookie sheet, about ¼ inch thick.

6. Bake in oven for 4 - 8 hours depending on your oven settings. When fruit is no longer sticky to touch remove from the oven.

7. If the fruit is still soft in the middle put the fruit covered parchment on a cooling rack and place the rack back on the pan. Put the pan back in the oven for another 1 or 2 hours so the bottom is completely dry, but not crispy.

8. Use a sharp knife or pizza cutter to cut the fruit leather into strips. Roll them up and wrap them in plastic wrap until you're ready to eat them.

. . . .

Option 2: Use left over Berry Sauce (page 35). If your sauce is very thick you can start with step 3. Otherwise go ahead and cook it in a saucepan for 5-10 minutes until it gets thicker.

. . . .

Option 3: Use any flavor of left over v(page 31). Start with step 1. Your fruit is already soft but it needs to get thick, so cook it for 10-20 minutes until it is reduced by half.

. . . .

Frank eats 5-8 servings of colorful fruits and vegetables every day. A serving is about the size of your fist.

BERRY SAUCE

This sweet fruity sauce is packed with berry flavor! I like it on pancakes and waffles and French toast and regular toast and... well, just about everything!

INGREDIENTS

⅓ cup low sugar dried pineapple

2 cups frozen berries, strawberries, blueberries etc.

DIRECTIONS

1. Place dried pineapple in the bottom of a medium sized bowl.

2. Place frozen strawberries on top of dried pineapple.

3. Cover and allow the berries to thaw on counter overnight or place in the microwave for 3-5 minutes.

4. Place all ingredients in blender and blend until smooth.

5. Adjust the sweetness by changing the amount of dried fruit you use.

Try This!

Left over Berry Sauce makes wonderful Rainbow Fruit Roll-Ups (page 33) or terrific Berry Applesauce (page 31). You can even use it on your Breakfast Banana Split (page 7).

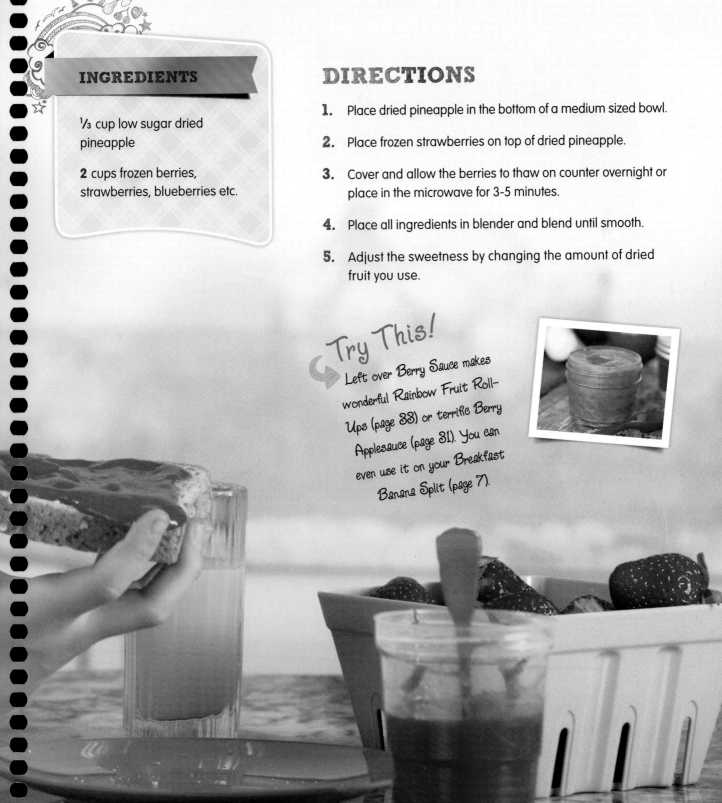

Foods look like the body part that they help. When you slice a carrot it looks kind of like the pupil of your eye. That can give you a hint that carrots are great for your eyes.

GLUTEN FREE!

INGREDIENTS

1 cucumber, peeled, seeded and cut into thick slices

2 large carrots, cut into coins

1 cup small broccoli florets

1 cup cauliflower florets

8 cherry tomatoes

4 wooden skewers

SALAD ON A STICK

Everything tastes better when it starts on a stick! Let's put our salad on a stick...it may be as good as a corndog!

DIRECTIONS

Gently thread the vegetables on the skewer, placing two or three pieces of each veggie on each skewer to make a pretty rainbow of colors.

INGREDIENTS

1 cup soy mayonnaise

½ cup Tofutti™ Sour Cream or additional soy mayonnaise

2 tablespoons lemon juice

2 teaspoons agave nectar or honey

½ teaspoon dried chives

½ teaspoon dried parsley

½ teaspoon dried dill weed

¼ teaspoon garlic powder

¼ teaspoon onion powder

⅛ teaspoon salt

RANCH DRESSING

DIRECTIONS

1. Mix all ingredients in a small bowl with a whisk until smooth.

2. Place in an airtight container and chill.

LUNCH BOX: This is a kidlicious way to add a couple of colors to your lunch. Put a little ranch dressing in a small cup for dip.

QUICK: Mix 2 tablespoons of Vegetarian Express Saucy Ranch seasoning mix into the Vegenaise and a little milk for a really quick ranch dressing.

Take these on a camping trip. Use aluminum foil to wrap them and then put them right into the coals for about 15 minutes to cook.

Color only counts if it is a natural color — the color that God gave it. Artificial colors like those in jellybeans do not have phytochemicals.

VEGGIE PRESENTS!

Presents for dinner! How cool is that! I love how everybody gets their very own little surprise to open at dinner time. The best part is they taste fantastic, but have lots of colors.

INGREDIENTS

1 medium zucchini

1 medium summer squash

2 cups red potatoes, diced

½ cup red bell pepper, diced

½ cup sweet onion, diced

2 tablespoons Italian dressing or **1** tablespoon olive oil

1 teaspoon minced garlic

1 teaspoon Italian seasoning

1-2 teaspoons salt to taste

DIRECTIONS

1. Preheat oven to 375°.

2. Clean and cut zucchini and summer squash into ½ to 1-inch-thick slices.

3. Clean potatoes by scrubbing with a brush and cut into cubes.

4. Clean red bell pepper and onion and cut into small pieces.

5. Place the prepared vegetables in a large mixing bowl and add the remaining ingredients. Stir the vegetables until well mixed.

6. Cut parchment paper or aluminum foil into 6-8 pieces, about 14 to 16 inches long.

7. Using one paper at a time, spray center of paper or foil with non-stick cooking spray. Spoon 1 to 1½ cups of the seasoned vegetables onto the parchment or foil.

8. Fold paper in half over vegetables. Starting at one edge roll the paper, moving around the edge to make a half moon shape. Tuck the end under and place on cookie sheet.

9. Bake the vegetables for 30 to 35 minutes.

10. Remove the presents from the oven and set them on a plate. Poke a hole or two at the top of each packet to allow the steam to escape. Wait about 5 minutes before opening the presents.

Try This!
Use spaghetti sauce in the veggies instead of the salad dressing.

SNEAKY GREEN ZUCCHINI PATTIES

You are absolutely going to LOVE these things! You can eat it in a sandwich or on the side with Stuffed Shells (page 95). Plus it adds green to your dinner and you don't even notice it!

INGREDIENTS

4 ½ cups zucchini, grated

2½-3 cups quick oats

1 cup cashew nuts, chopped small

5 tablespoons chicken style seasoning

1 teaspoon salt

¼ cup gluten flour

3 tablespoons nutritional yeast flakes

1-2 medium onions, diced fine

DIRECTIONS

1. Preheat oven to 350°. Prepare baking sheet by spraying with non-stick cooking spray.

2. Mix all ingredients together in a large bowl. You should be able to press them together into patties. If more moisture is needed, add a little olive oil. If mixture is too moist add a few more oats.

3. Make into burger-shaped patties and place on cookie sheet and spray with non-stick cooking spray. Bake for 20 minutes. Flip the patties over and spray again. Bake 15 minutes on the other side.

LUNCH BOX: Zucchini patties are perfect for packing in your lunch. You can serve them in a sandwich or on their own with a little tomato sauce for dipping.

Freeze leftover patties for a quick side dish or sandwich.

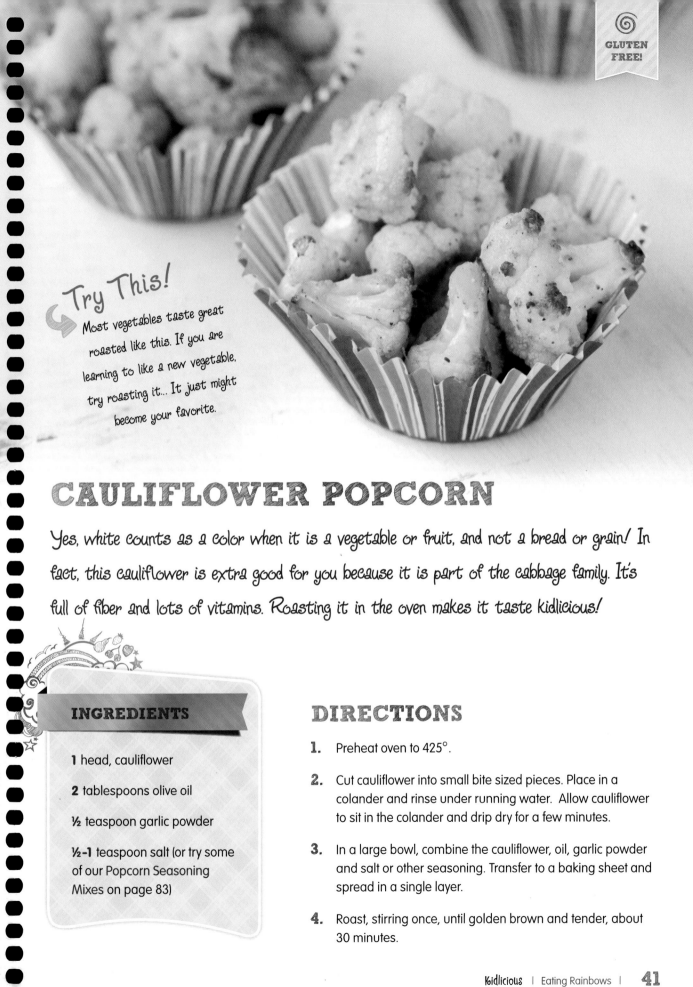

Try This!

Most vegetables taste great roasted like this. If you are learning to like a new vegetable, try roasting it... It just might become your favorite.

CAULIFLOWER POPCORN

Yes, white counts as a color when it is a vegetable or fruit, and not a bread or grain! In fact, this cauliflower is extra good for you because it is part of the cabbage family. It's full of fiber and lots of vitamins. Roasting it in the oven makes it taste kidlicious!

INGREDIENTS

1 head, cauliflower

2 tablespoons olive oil

½ teaspoon garlic powder

½-1 teaspoon salt (or try some of our Popcorn Seasoning Mixes on page 83)

DIRECTIONS

1. Preheat oven to 425°.

2. Cut cauliflower into small bite sized pieces. Place in a colander and rinse under running water. Allow cauliflower to sit in the colander and drip dry for a few minutes.

3. In a large bowl, combine the cauliflower, oil, garlic powder and salt or other seasoning. Transfer to a baking sheet and spread in a single layer.

4. Roast, stirring once, until golden brown and tender, about 30 minutes.

EDAMAME MUNCHIES

Amazing, little treats that are excellent for any lunch box. Edamames are little green soybeans, so they are full of protein and extraordinarily good when roasted in the oven. They start out green and then turn brown... maybe they can count for two colors!

INGREDIENTS

2 cups frozen edamame

1 tablespoon olive oil

1 teaspoon salt

1 teaspoon garlic powder

Pinch cayenne pepper (optional)

DIRECTIONS

1. Preheat oven to 375°.

2. Place beans in a colander and rinse under warm water.

3. Place them on a "bed" of paper towels and dry them with another paper towel on top.

4. Place edamames in a medium sized bowl, drizzle with oil.

5. Sprinkle with salt, garlic and cayenne, if using. Mix well.

6. Spread in a single layer on a small cookie sheet and bake for 30 to 35 minutes, stirring once or twice, until beans are completely dry and crunchy.

LUNCH BOX: Better than chips, they are salty and crunchy and super healthy!

BAKED KALE CHIPS

GLUTEN FREE!

Love 'em! They are crispy and salty like chips are supposed to be, AND they are green!

INGREDIENTS

1 bunch kale

1 tablespoon olive oil

1 teaspoon salt

1 teaspoon garlic powder

1 teaspoon onion powder

Pinch cayenne pepper (optional)

DIRECTIONS

1. Preheat oven to 350°. Line a non-insulated cookie sheet with parchment paper.

2. Wash kale and remove stems and tear into chip size pieces.

3. Spread on paper towels to let air dry. If you have a salad spinner this is a great time to use it.

4. Place kale in a large bowl and drizzle with olive oil and sprinkle with salt, garlic, onion and cayenne, if using.

5. Mix with hands and gently rub kale until every leaf is coated.

6. Bake for 10 - 15 minutes, until dry and crispy and the edges turn a little brown.

The trick to making these come out great is making sure the leaves are completely dry before you put them in the oven. Otherwise they will steam instead of dry, and get soft instead of crunchy.

Chips For a Friend

Do you have a teacher or friend you would like to surprise with a little gift? Why not make this cute froggie and fill it with Kale Chips for a fun gift.

Kale Chips

Once Frank tried Brussels sprouts and thought that they did not taste so good. But, he decided he would learn to like them. And he did, all he had to do was to try a bite or two every time mom made them.

RAINBOW SOUP

Every color of the rainbow...it's in there!

INGREDIENTS

2 large potatoes, diced

1 onion diced

1-28 ounce can petite diced tomatoes

1-1 pound bag frozen mixed vegetables

1 cup purple cabbage diced

½ cup carrots diced

2 stalks celery diced

2 tablespoons beef like seasoning or chicken style seasoning

1 tablespoon salt

½ teaspoon basil

1 teaspoon dill weed

¼ teaspoon celery seed

water to cover vegetables

¾ cup ABC pasta (or other small fun shape)

DIRECTIONS

1. Add all ingredients except pasta to a large soup pan.

2. Bring to a boil and reduce heat to medium, cover and let cook for 30 minutes.

3. Add pasta and cook for 4-5 minutes until pasta is done.

LUNCH BOX: Rainbow soup is great to pack in your lunch with a Kidliciable (page 69) or even a sandwich for a perfect hot lunch on a really cold day.

Instead of an electric mixer for mashed potatoes, you can use a potato masher. Just don't put them in the food processor or they will turn into glue...I tried it.

Potatoes have vitamin C, potassium, vitamin B6, they have a lot of energy packed into them that help you feel fuller longer.

GLUTEN FREE!

INGREDIENTS

12 small to medium whole red potatoes

3 tablespoons olive oil

1 teaspoon garlic powder

1 teaspoon onion powder

Salt to taste

Try This!

Great for breakfast. Boil the potatoes the night before and bake them in the morning while you're getting ready for school!

INGREDIENTS

5 pounds russet potatoes, peeled and diced

2 teaspoons salt, divided

1 ½ cups non-dairy unsweetened milk

2 tablespoons non-hydrogenated soy margarine

SMASHED POTATOES

Almost better than French fries! That's very hard to believe, I know.. you'll just have to try them to find out.

DIRECTIONS

1. Preheat oven to 450°. Line a cookie sheet with parchment paper and drizzle with a little oil.

2. Bring a large pot of salted water to a boil. Add potatoes and cook until they are soft when you poke them with a fork.

4. Place boiled potatoes on cookie sheet, leaving some space between each potato.

5. With a potato masher or heavy cup, gently press down each potato until it looks smashed. Drizzle with oil and sprinkle with salt, garlic powder and onion powder.

6. Bake for 20-25 minutes until golden brown.

MASHED POTATOES

I think daddy would eat mashed potatoes every day if we would make them.

DIRECTIONS

1. Place peeled and diced potatoes in a large pot and cover with water.

2. Add 1 teaspoon salt to water and bring to a boil.

3. Reduce heat and let simmer for 15-20 minutes until potatoes are very soft and fall apart when poked with a fork.

4. Have an adult helper drain the water out of the pan.

5. Add non-dairy unsweetened milk and margarine.

6. Using an electric mixer, whip the potatoes for several minutes until the potatoes are fluffy and all of the lumps are gone.

MYSTERY IN THE CLASSROOM

CASE #3:

The Stomach That Never Gets Full

Case Notes: It seems like Logan is always hungry. He eats lunch and feels full, but an hour later he is hungry again. He feels so tired that he can't concentrate. We need to help him figure out what's wrong so he can have more fun at school and get better grades.

 Watch for clues!

Interview Transcript:

Investigator: Tell me, Logan, what do you usually eat for lunch?

Logan: I always have bologna and cheese on white bread, chips, cookies and an apple.

Investigator: Do you eat all of your lunch?

Logan: After I eat everything else, I am usually too full to eat the apple.

Investigator: So you feel full after lunch?

Logan: Yes, but by the time we start science class, I am hungry and sleepy.

Investigator: The only thing in your lunch with fiber is the apple, and you don't eat that. I wonder if fiber can help solve this problem. Let's investigate!

Evidence:

- Logan eats his lunch but it does not keep him satisfied.

- Logan gets tired after lunch.

- Logan's lunch does not have fiber.

THE VERDICT

When Logan eats high fiber foods he has more energy and doesn't get hungry right after he eats. That means he can think better and get better grades in school!

Thinking
Outside the...
Lunch Box

Eating high fiber foods helps your body and your brain have the energy it needs for the next 4-6 hours.

Look for the vegetarian lunchmeat and non-dairy cheese slices in the produce department of your local grocery store, next to the tofu. If your market does not carry them,, you can find them at the health food store.

Deli Sandwich

2 slices whole grain sandwich bread

2 teaspoons soy mayonnaise

2 slices vegetarian lunchmeat

2 romaine lettuce leaves

4 Refrigerator Dill Pickles (page 137)

2 slices tomato

1 slice onion

Tex Mex Sandwich

1 whole grain burger bun

1 tablespoon prepared guacamole

1 Black Bean Slider (page 97) or a burger from the store

2 tomato slices

3 tablespoon spicy sprouts

Veggie Meatloaf

2 slices whole grain bread

2 teaspoons soy mayonnaise

2 slices leftover Meatloaf (page 93)

2 leaves romaine lettuce

2 slices tomato

1 slice onion (optional)

3 slices Bread and Butter Pickles (page 137)

SANDWICH LUNCHES

Sandwiches are the main attraction in a traditional lunch box. I LOVE sandwiches because there are so many different kinds. You could probably try a new sandwich every week for the whole school year!

DIRECTIONS

1. Spread bread with spread (soy mayonnaise or guacamole).

2. Layer remaining ingredients on one slice of bread.

3. Put the remaining slice of bread on top.

4. Place sandwich in a reusable sandwich container or wrap in wax paper and pack in your lunch box.

FUN LUNCH: Do you love jokes and riddles? Ask your mom or dad (even a brother or sister) to put a silly joke or riddle in your lunch box. Share your riddle with friends over the lunch table.

I LOVE YOU

Beans are a really good source of fiber.

SANDWICH SPREADS

Sandwich spreads are a good way to make sandwiches quickly and easily. Everything you need is right in the spread. I like to make spreads out of tofu, garbanzo beans, or vegetarian hot dogs. They all make a fantastic sandwich! Also, they are really good on crackers for a Kidliciable style lunch (page 69).

INGREDIENTS

1 package (14 ounce) extra firm tofu, OR 1 can (15 ounce) garbanzo beans, drained, OR 1 package vegetarian hotdogs

1 stalk celery, finely diced

¼ cup sweet pickle relish or Bread and Butter Pickles (page 137), finely diced

¼ cup soy mayonnaise

2 tablespoons sweet onion, finely diced

1 tablespoon chicken style seasoning (omit when using vegetarian hotdogs)

¾ teaspoon garlic powder

½ teaspoon onion powder

½ - ¾ teaspoon salt

DIRECTIONS

1. If using tofu, drain water and wrap tightly in 2 clean dry dishtowels and let sit for 20-30 minutes, to remove excess moisture.

2. Mash drained tofu or garbanzo beans or hot dogs in a large bowl with a fork or potato masher. A food processor works well also.

3. Add remaining ingredients and mix well. Chill before serving.

FUN LUNCH: Make a secret message banana! Use a toothpick to write a note on a banana. You won't be able to see the writing right away, but after a couple of hours your message will appear.

Try This!

If you are serving lunch to friends at home, make it special with a tomato flower. Starting at the top of the tomato, cut it into wedges but don't cut all the way through. When you put it on the plate, the tomato will lay open to make the petals of the flower. Now put a spoonful of the sandwich spread in the middle, and you have a beautiful flower. See how on www.kidlicious.com.

Look for the vegetarian lunchmeat in the produce department of your local grocery store, next to the tofu. If your market does not carry it, then you can find it at the health food store.

If you choose a lunch that includes whole grain bread, vegetables, beans, nuts and fruit you will have plenty of fiber.

INGREDIENTS

1 whole-grain sandwich wrap or tortilla

1 tablespoon Vegenaise or other cholesterol free mayonnaise

3 vegetarian turkey deli slices

1 small handful spinach leaves

1-2 tablespoons dried cranberries

THANKSGIVING WRAP

Thanksgiving is one of my favorite holidays. It's fun to go to Grandma's house and see all of the cousins. It's also fun to remember the blessings we have been given through the year. One thing I am thankful for is having Thanksgiving dinner in my lunch box more than once a year.

DIRECTIONS

1. Heat tortilla in microwave for 10 seconds.
2. Spread soy mayonnaise on one side of wrap or tortilla.
3. Layer on vegetarian turkey slices, spinach, and dried cranberries.
4. Roll tightly into a wrap.
5. Serve with your favorite fruit or vegetable.

INGREDIENTS

2 teaspoons Ranch Dressing (page 37) or BBQ sauce

1 small handful lettuce, shredded

2 tablespoons tomato, diced

1 (6-inch) whole grain tortilla

4 Wonder Nuggets (page 101)

NUGGET WRAP

DIRECTIONS

1. Mix ranch dressing or BBQ sauce with the lettuce and tomato.
2. Place wonder nuggets down the center of the tortilla.
3. Add the lettuce and tomato mixture.
4. Eat like a soft taco.

FUN LUNCH: Brightly colored napkins make the lunch box a happier place. Look for them on clearance after holidays.

You can use The "B" in many different recipes. Try it in the BLT Pasta Salad (page 79), or with your Scrambled Tofu (page 17). It is a good idea to keep some in the freezer. You can pull it out when you need a quick and easy lunch.

Pancake syrup does not work for this recipe; use only the real maple syrup.

INGREDIENTS

1 large whole wheat tortilla

1 tablespoon soy mayonnaise (optional)

3 slices tomato

¼ cup The "B" (recipe below)

2 leaves romaine lettuce, shredded

¼ avocado, diced and sprinkled with lemon juice (the juice keeps the avocado from turning brown)

INGREDIENTS

1 tablespoon olive oil

3 cups soy curls

3 tablespoons Bragg's® Liquid Aminos or low-sodium soy sauce

2 tablespoons liquid smoke, hickory flavor

¼ teaspoon salt, optional

¼-½ teaspoon cayenne pepper

3-4 tablespoons pure maple syrup

BLAT WRAP

Do BLATs grow on trees? Is it some new vegetable? No, a BLAT is a sandwich people usually make with bacon, lettuce and tomato. They call it a BLT. I like to make my "B" out of soy curls, and add Avocado for the "A". B-L-A-T!

DIRECTIONS

1. Warm tortilla in the microwave for 10-20 seconds. This makes it easier to roll up.

2. Spread soy mayonnaise over the tortilla.

3. Arrange thin slices of tomato.

4. Place ¼ cup of "B" over the tomato.

5. Top with shredded lettuce and diced avocado.

6. Wrap "burrito style".

THE "B"

I love creating new recipes! I usually change things up and make them a little different just for fun. This recipe was inspired by a great cookbook called Vegan Diner by Julie Hasson.

DIRECTIONS

1. Soak soy curls in hot water for 10 minutes. Drain off liquid.

2. Heat oil in non-stick skillet. Add soy curls and sauté for 2 minutes.

3. Mix Bragg's®, liquid smoke, salt and cayenne together in a small bowl. Pour over soy curls, stirring well to make sure all the soy curls are coated.

4. Cook until browned, about 8-10 minutes stirring occasionally. I like them very brown and even a little crispy.

5. Drizzle maple syrup over soy curls and stir well. Continue cooking for 2-3 more minutes.

BREAKFAST FOR LUNCH BURRITO

Next time you have scrambled tofu and potatoes for breakfast, save a little for a lunch later in the week. Or you can make the tofu ahead and freeze it for later. Just don't try freezing those potatoes!

INGREDIENTS

1 whole grain tortilla

⅓ cup Scrambled Tofu (page 17)

1 small Smashed Potatoes (page 47)

1 tablespoon salsa or Real Tomato Ketchup (page 139)

DIRECTIONS

1. Warm tortilla in the microwave for 10-20 seconds. This makes it easier to roll up.

2. Place tofu down the center of the tortilla.

3. Chop Smashed Potatoes and place on top of the tofu.

4. Add a little salsa or homemade ketchup.

5. Roll it up "burrito style" and wrap in wax paper or parchment paper.

If you have a little of The "B" (page 57) leftover, it would be very tasty in this burrito too.

FUN LUNCH: Around Easter time you can find little plastic balls that are hollow, and you can hide surprises inside. They are perfect for lunch box notes or hidden treats.

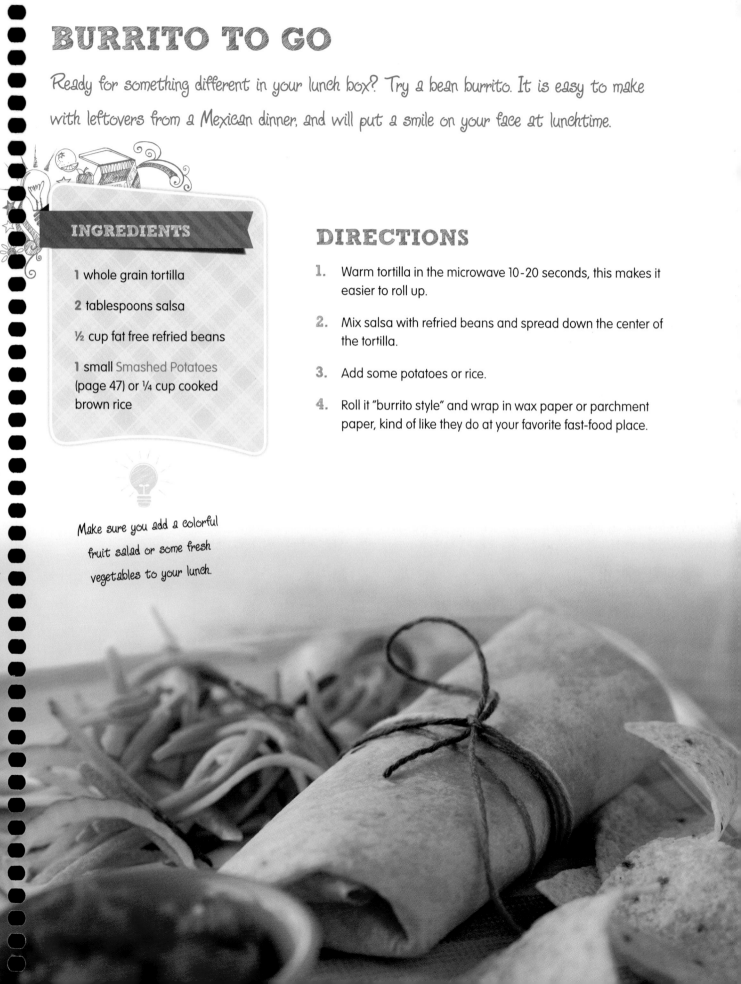

BURRITO TO GO

Ready for something different in your lunch box? Try a bean burrito. It is easy to make with leftovers from a Mexican dinner, and will put a smile on your face at lunchtime.

INGREDIENTS

1 whole grain tortilla

2 tablespoons salsa

½ cup fat free refried beans

1 small Smashed Potatoes (page 47) or ¼ cup cooked brown rice

DIRECTIONS

1. Warm tortilla in the microwave 10-20 seconds, this makes it easier to roll up.

2. Mix salsa with refried beans and spread down the center of the tortilla.

3. Add some potatoes or rice.

4. Roll it "burrito style" and wrap in wax paper or parchment paper, kind of like they do at your favorite fast-food place.

Make sure you add a colorful fruit salad or some fresh vegetables to your lunch.

Look for the vegetarian hotdogs or lunchmeat in the produce department of your local grocery store, next to the tofu. If your market does not carry them, you can find them at the health food store.

Oatmeal has 6 grams of fiber per cup. Try to find a cereal that has at least 3 – 5 grams of fiber per serving.

SANDWICH ON A STICK

When I get Sandwich on a Stick in my lunch box, my friends are so jealous!

INGREDIENTS

2 slices soft whole grain bread

1 tablespoon favorite sandwich spread (ketchup, soy mayonnaise, etc.)

2 vegetarian hotdogs or 4 slices vegetarian lunchmeat

8 Refrigerator Pickles (page 137)

8 grape or cherry tomatoes

4 bamboo skewers

DIRECTIONS

1. Spread sandwich spread on bread.

2. Cut each slice of bread into 6 pieces.

3. Cut hot dogs into 4 pieces each or cut lunchmeat slices in half.

4. Thread ingredients on skewers in the following order: bread, hotdog, pickle, tomato, bread, hotdog, pickle, tomato, bread.

5. Repeat with remaining skewers.

Try This!
Wonder Nuggets (page 101) left over from supper work great on these sandwich sticks.

FUN LUNCH: We have Smoothies (page 131) at least once a week and there is usually just a little left over. I put it in a small plastic container with a tight lid and put it in the freezer. Later, I put it in my lunch box for a special treat! It keeps my lunch cold, and it is thawed enough to eat by lunch time!

Tips for a Great Sandwich Lunch

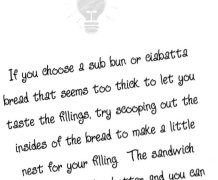

If you choose a sub bun or ciabatta bread that seems too thick to let you taste the fillings, try scooping out the insides of the bread to make a little nest for your filling. The sandwich will stay together better and you can taste all the yummy goodness.

Change Up Your Bread

Even PB & J tastes better when you change up the bread! Try using a tortilla, bagel, English muffin, or sub bun. You could even get a little fancy and have some ciabatta bread. But if you want to go really crazy, use a waffle for your bread! I wonder what your friends will think of that?

Whatever bread you choose, make sure it has whole grain flour as the first ingredient. Also check to see that it has at least 3 grams of fiber. (Check out page 155 for more information about how to read a label).

Spread it thin!

Every great sandwich has a great spread. Soy mayonnaise, ketchup, mustard, guacamole or a little of your favorite salad dressing are all good on your sandwich. Just be careful! These sauces are not meant to take over the sandwich…a little goes a long way.

If you are using a salad dressing, mix it in with the lettuce or greens before adding it to the sandwich. That way you can get the flavor all the way through, and it is less likely to leak out.

Fill it up!

When you fill up your sandwich, make sure you choose something with protein that will help you grow strong! Tofu, bean spreads like hummus, nut butters, or vegetarian lunchmeat slices are all high in protein.

Add some color and crunch to your sandwich with vegetables like lettuce, cucumber slices, onions, tomatoes, shredded carrots, shredded peppers, or even avocado slices.

If you are using a tortilla or flat bread to make a wrap, warm it up for about 10 seconds in the microwave so it rolls more easily and doesn't crack.

An easy way to make a sandwich more fun is to cut it into different shapes.

Avoid a soggy sandwich by packing veggies like lettuce, tomato, and onion in a separate container. Put the sandwich together at school.

Look for the vegetarian lunchmeat and non-dairy cheese slices in the produce department of your local grocery store, next to the tofu. If your market does not carry them then you can find them at the health food store.

Bologna Pinwheels

1 lavash bread or **2** (6 inch) whole grain tortillas

2 tablespoons soy mayonnaise

4 slices vegetarian lunchmeat, bologna flavor

2 slices American-flavored non-dairy cheese alternative

4 lettuce leaves

Rainbow Veggie Pinwheels

1 lavash bread or **2** (6 inch) whole grain flour tortillas

3 tablespoons soy cream cheese, French onion or chive flavor

1 handful of rainbow salad mix (available in the produce isle of the grocery store)

2 green onions, thinly sliced

Peanut Butter & Fruit

1 lavash bread or **2** whole grain flour tortillas

3 tablespoons peanut butter

¼ cup sliced fruit (apples, bananas, grapes, strawberries)

2 tablespoons dried fruit (raisins, dates, etc.)

PINWHEEL SANDWICHES

In a pinwheel, everything is laid out flat, then it is rolled up into a tight little roll. It looks really cool and comes in fun bite sized pieces.

DIRECTIONS

1. Spread soy mayonnaise, soy cream cheese or peanut butter evenly onto tortillas or lavash bread, making sure to take it all the way to the edge.

2. Layer each of the remaining ingredients in a thin layer over tortilla or lavash bread.

3. Starting at one end, roll tortilla or lavash bread tightly away from you. Wrap individually in plastic wrap, and chill.

4. In the morning, cut the rolls into slices to create pinwheels.

FUN LUNCH: Fun butterflies can greet you in your lunch box! All you need is a clothes pin, a pipe cleaner, glue to attach the pipe cleaners, markers to make eyes, and a small bag for little treats you want to put in your lunch box! **www.kidlicious.com**

A great, fiber rich breakfast includes whole grain cereal, at least 2 servings of fruits, some nuts or nut butter, whole grain bread, and non-dairy milk.

PIZZA ROLLS

The ultimate pinwheel sandwich! Pizza!

INGREDIENTS

⅓ recipe Oatmeal Bread Dough (page 141) or frozen pizza dough

¼ cup basil pesto

½ cup favorite pizza toppings (olives, onions, peppers, mushrooms, tomatoes, sundried tomatoes, vegetarian sausage or pepperoni, etc.)

¼ cup non-dairy mozzarella cheese (optional)

1 cup tomato sauce or pizza sauce

Go to Kidlicious.com for a really yummy dairy-free Basil and Walnut Pesto recipe.

DIRECTIONS

1. Preheat oven to 350° and line a cookie sheet with parchment paper.

2. Cover the dough ball with a damp towel and allow the dough to rest for 15 minutes. This helps the gluten in the dough to relax and makes it easier to work with.

3. Sprinkle a little flour on the counter and on a rolling pin to prevent dough from sticking. Use the rolling pin to roll the dough into a rectangle about ⅛ inch thick.

4. Spread basil pesto over dough, leaving an inch or two uncovered at one of the long ends. Sprinkle a few favorite toppings and non-dairy cheese over the pesto.

5. Starting at the long end that is covered with yummy toppings, roll the dough gently but tightly toward the other end, just like a jellyroll. Pinch the dough together at the end to seal.

6. Using a sharp knife, cut the roll into 1-inch rounds, using a sawing motion. Place on a parchment-lined baking sheet about an inch apart. Cover rolls with a clean dishtowel and let rise for 10 minutes.

7. Spray tops with non-stick cooking spray and bake for 25 - 30 minutes.

8. Serve with tomato sauce or pizza sauce for dipping.

FUN LUNCH: Did you know? In 1820, a tomato was considered a juicy red KILLER! Ask your mom to put an amazing fact in your lunch box. There are several books full of cool stuff available from **www.amazingfacts.com**.

KIDLICIABLE
SANDWICH STYLE

A lot of kids love the little packaged lunches that have separate compartments filled with different items for stacking or dipping. It's even more fun to make your own! You can use lots more colors and choose whole grain bread and crackers. I like to eat my Kidliciables with a thermos full of soup to make my lunch complete.

INGREDIENTS

8-10 whole grain crackers

3 vegetarian lunchmeat slices, cut into fourths

2 non-dairy soy cheese slices, cut into fourths

2 stalks celery, cut into sticks

2 tablespoons peanut butter or Ranch Dressing (page 37)

1 Rainbow Fruit-Roll Ups (page 33)

DIRECTIONS

1. Put each ingredient into an individual container and create your sandwiches at the lunch table.

GLUTEN FREE There is a variety of delicious gluten free crackers. That makes homemade Kidliciables a perfect lunch for those who can't eat gluten.

Using non-dairy cheese slices in a Kidliciable can be a little tricky because they are softer than dairy cheese slices. Leave the plastic wrap on and have a grown-up use a sharp knife to cut the slices into fourths. You'll have a small, stackable size without getting them all squished together.

Whole grain bread has fiber that fills you up and keeps you feeling full longer. Choose bread that has at least 3 grams of fiber. (see page 155).

INGREDIENTS

½ cup fat free refried beans

¼ cup lettuce, shredded

2 tablespoons tomato, diced

2 tablespoons black olives, sliced

2 tablespoons non-dairy sour cream

1 handful tortilla chips

1 whole grain tortilla, cut into four pieces

1 Chunky Monkey (page 119)

MEXICAN STYLE KIDLICIABLES

What's better than Mexican food in your lunch?

Yeah, I can't think of anything either.

DIRECTIONS

1. Place each ingredient in a small container and build your own taco or nacho at lunchtime.

FUN LUNCH: Cut the apple in the morning, being careful to keep all of the pieces together. Use a rubber band to hold it together and put it in your lunch box. It won't turn brown, and now it is perfect for dipping.

INGREDIENTS

1/3 cup Sandwich spread (page 53)

8-10 whole grain crackers or pita triangles

Cut vegetables (carrots, peppers, cauliflower etc.)

2 tablespoons ranch dressing

1 apple, sliced

4 tablespoons peanut butter, for dipping

DIPPING STYLE KIDLICIABLES

I love taking my lunch for a dip!

DIRECTIONS

1. Put each ingredient into an individual container and dip your crackers, pita, and veggies for a fun dipping style lunch.

 GLUTEN FREE There is a variety of delicious gluten free crackers which make homemade Kidliciables a perfect lunch for those who can't eat gluten.

KIDLICIABLE PIZZA

Pizza is good any way you slice it, and even if you don't slice it! Like with Pizza Kidliciables!

INGREDIENTS

2 mini whole wheat pita breads or English muffins (whole grain crackers are good too)

¼ cup pizza sauce

2 or 3 small containers with favorite pizza toppings

1 small container mandarin oranges, drained and rinsed (this helps reduce the added sugar in which they are usually packaged)

DIRECTIONS

1. Put each ingredient into an individual container and you can build your own little pizzas at lunchtime.

Topping Ideas

- Onions
- Green peppers
- Banana peppers
- Jalapeño peppers
- Fresh basil
- Black olives
- Green olives
- Mushrooms
- Pineapple
- Tomatoes
- Spinach
- Artichoke hearts
- Sundried tomatoes
- Veggie pepperoni
- Sausage crumbles
- Non-dairy cheese shreds or slices

FUN LUNCH: Keep some small plastic containers on hand. Whenever you make applesauce or open a can of fruit, fill a bunch of your containers and put them in the freezer. Move one to the fridge the night before you want it in your lunch box.

GLUTEN FREE It's easy to find gluten free crackers so this is a great way to eat pizza if you can't have gluten!

LEFTOVERS FOR LUNCH

Anything you had for breakfast or supper can easily make a great lunch. Here are some menu ideas to get you packing.

Mac & Cheese

Mac & Cheese needs no introduction! It is always good for lunch or for dinner…maybe even breakfast!

Mac & Cheese (page 99)

Broccoli & baby carrots with ranch dip

Baked beans

Frozen Smoothie (page 131)

Cincinnati Chili

A different way to eat up that leftover Colorful Chili from supper is to have it over spaghetti noodles. It may sound a little strange, but my dad says people do it all the time in Ohio.

Colorful Chili (page 105)

Spaghetti Noodles

Salad on a Stick with Ranch Dressing (page 37)

FUN LUNCH: A thermos is a "must have" if you are going to eat those leftovers for lunch. It will keep your food hot for hours. All you have to do is put your food in a glass bowl in the microwave while you are eating breakfast. Pour the hot food into the thermos and put it in your lunch box.

Stroganoff with Noodles

Daddy ate all the mashed potatoes at supper so how am I going to have stroganoff in my lunch box? Noodles! That's perfect!

Stroganoff (page 103)

Noodles

Salad on a Stick (page 37)

Fruit Cup (page 73 Fun Lunch tip)

Look for lunch box tips everywhere in this book to learn other great ways to fill your lunch box with stuff you already cooked!

If using frozen edamame, put
them in the pasta for the
last minute of cooking.

Meats, cheeses and other dairy products don't have any fiber.

ASIAN NOODLE SALAD

Bright and colorful veggies mixed with noodles...who doesn't like noodles! Oh, and the peanut sauce...yes peanut butter does tastes good on *EVERYTHING!*

INGREDIENTS

1 package (14 ounce) cubed firm tofu

¼ cup Bragg's® Liquid Aminos or low-sodium soy sauce

10 ounces whole wheat spaghetti noodles or rice noodles

1 cup shelled edamame, fresh or frozen

⅓ cup red bell pepper, sliced thin

⅓ cup purple cabbage, sliced thin

⅓ cup carrots, shredded

¼ cup green onion, diced small.

....

Dressing

¼ cup peanut butter

¼ cup vegetable broth or ¼ cup water and 1 teaspoon chicken-style seasoning.

2 tablespoons Bragg's® Liquid Aminos or low-sodium soy sauce

1 tablespoon toasted sesame oil

1 tablespoon lemon juice

2 teaspoons honey or agave nectar

2 cloves garlic, minced

2 teaspoons ginger, minced or grated

DIRECTIONS

1. Drain water from tofu and wrap tightly in 2 clean dry dishtowels and let sit for 20-30 minutes to remove excess moisture.

2. Cut tofu into one-inch cubes and place in a shallow dish. Pour Bragg's® or soy sauce over the cubes. Allow the tofu to soak for about 10 minutes. This is called marinating.

3. Cook noodles according to package instructions. Drain and rinse under cold water.

4. Heat a dry non-stick skillet over medium heat, drain tofu and add to hot skillet stirring occasionally, until all sides are browned.

5. Add the noodles to a large bowl with the edamame, bell pepper, cabbage, carrots, green onion and cooked tofu.

6. Mix dressing ingredients in a small glass bowl. If you are having trouble mixing in the peanut butter you can place it in the microwave for 30-60 seconds and it will be easier to mix.

7. Pour dressing over the noodles and toss to combine.

8. Serve cold just as it is, or you can warm it up a little if you like.

....

FUN LUNCH: Instead of plain old silverware for lunch pack some fun utensils like small forks or a spork which is a fork and spoon in one. Even chopsticks will make lunch a little more interesting.

Fiber is found in foods that we eat just the way God made them. Beans, vegetables, and fruits all have fiber. Whole grain breads and cereals also have fiber.

BLT PASTA SALAD

Pasta salad is always a favorite, but this pasta salad is a meal, and it is crazy good! We made this recipe big enough to share with the whole family. But make sure to save some out for your lunch or there may not be any left!

INGREDIENTS

1 package (7 ounces) whole grain or fiber-added pasta

1½ cups The "B" (page 57)

4 cups hearts of romaine, thinly sliced and cut into bite sized pieces

2 Roma tomatoes, seeded and chopped

¼ cup purple cabbage, shredded

¼ cup green onion, sliced

Dressing

¾ cup soy mayonnaise

¼ cup lemon juice

2 teaspoons cane juice crystals

2 teaspoons chicken-style seasoning

DIRECTIONS

1. Cook noodles according to package instructions. Drain and rinse under cold water.

2. In a large bowl, mix pasta with remaining ingredients, except dressing.

3. In a separate small bowl, mix all dressing ingredients.

4. Before serving, pour dressing over salad and mix well.

LUNCH BOX: Mission of the week: Go undercover as a secret agent, doing good deeds around your school. Ask your mom, dad, brother or sister to help you make a list of good deeds you can do. Write each one on a separate piece of paper, and fold it up. Put them in a jar and pull one out each week. Stick it in your lunch box for a mid-day surprise!

GLUTEN FREE Use gluten free pasta for an amazing gluten free treat!

QUICK: Skip the burger and beans and use 2-3 cups of leftover Colorful Chili (page 105) or use canned chili beans.

WALKING TACO

A lot of you have had a walking taco. Some of you call it a taco salad or a haystack. Whatever the name, it sure tastes good! You can make this for dinner and then make it a walking taco by taking it to school with you for your lunch box.

INGREDIENTS

2 tablespoons oil

1 sweet onion, diced

1 package (12 ounces) vegetarian burger substitute or 2 cups Walnut Gluten, ground (page 135)

1 package taco seasoning mix

5 cups romaine lettuce, shredded (about 1 large head)

1 cup baby spinach, shredded

1 can red kidney beans, rinsed and drained

1-2 tomatoes, diced

4 green onions, sliced

¼ cup yellow pepper, diced small

1 cup non-dairy cheese alternative (optional)

2 cups corn chips or tortilla chips, coarsely crushed

¼ cup Ranch Dressing (page 37)

DIRECTIONS

1. Heat oil in a large skillet over medium high heat.

2. Add oil, onion, and vegetarian burger. Cook until burger is browned and onions are translucent (almost clear) about 5-6 minutes.

3. Add taco seasoning and mix well. You can add a couple of tablespoons of water if your burger starts to stick and you need it to help mix in the taco seasoning. When cooked, set burger and onions aside to cool.

4. In a large bowl, add lettuce, spinach, beans, tomatoes, onions, pepper, cheese (optional), chips, and burger.

5. Add Ranch Dressing and mix one more time before serving.

LUNCH BOX: Before you mix it together for the family, pack a little vegetarian burger and beans in a container large enough to hold all of the ingredients. Pack some of the veggies and chips in separate baggies. Just dump it all together when the lunch bell rings. Your chips will still be crisp, and your lunch will be Kidlicious!

 GLUTEN FREE Use a soy-based burger substitute like TVP or simply use seasoned chili beans to replace it.

HOMEMADE MICROWAVE POPCORN

Did you know? You can make your own super easy microwave popcorn with just a paper bag and popcorn kernels! Not only is it cheaper than the stuff you can buy at the store but it doesn't have a lot of weird ingredients. Now that is Kidlicious!

INGREDIENTS

1 brown paper lunch bag

¼ cup popcorn kernels

Popcorn seasoning

DIRECTIONS

1. Place popcorn kernels in bag and fold the top over twice.

2. Microwave on high for about 3 minutes. When the popping slows down take it out of the microwave.

3. Season with popcorn seasoning of your choice.

LUNCH BOX: We all love popcorn, but we often forget about it when we are packing our lunches. It is way better than chips and it has lots of fiber!

POPCORN SEASONINGS

Mix up a batch of seasonings to keep on hand whenever you're in the mood for popcorn. Blending up your seasoning mix helps the seasoning stick to the popcorn instead of falling to the bottom of the bowl.

Kidlicious Popcorn Seasoning

1 cup nutritional yeast flakes

¼ cup salt

Italian Popcorn Seasoning

½ cup nutritional yeast flakes

2 tablespoons salt

½ tablespoon oregano

1 tablespoon basil

Southwestern Popcorn Seasoning

¼ cup chili powder

¼ cup nutritional yeast flakes

¼ cup salt

1 tablespoon ground cumin

1 tablespoon onion powder

1 tablespoon garlic powder

1-1½ teaspoons cayenne pepper (optional)

Dilly Popcorn Seasoning

¼ cup onion powder

¼ cup garlic powder

¼ cup salt

½ cup nutritional yeast flakes

¼ cup dill weed

DIRECTIONS

1. Place in a dry blender and blend to a powder.

2. Pour into a shaker and sprinkle as much or as little as you like.

Popcorn Gift

Share the lessons you have learned from popcorn with someone who needs them. Make this fun gift pail, and fill it with popcorn and seasonings to give to someone who needs it. Don't forget to print off a copy of Lessons From Popcorn to share too! **www.kidlicious.com**

LESSONS FROM POPCORN

When you give your life to Jesus, you become a brand new person. You can read about it in 2 Corinthians 5:17.

Heat
Without the heat we can never have the fluffy white popcorn we want. It is the same in life. Heat shows us that God uses the trials and life experiences we go through to help us grow more and more like Jesus (1 Peter 4:12-13).

No Black Pepper on Popcorn
We want to stay far away from sins that make us dirty (Daniel 1:8).

The Pan
All the kernels gather together in the pan to become popcorn, just like Christians should gather together in the Church so that we can work together to become all that God wants us to be (1 Corinthians 12:12).

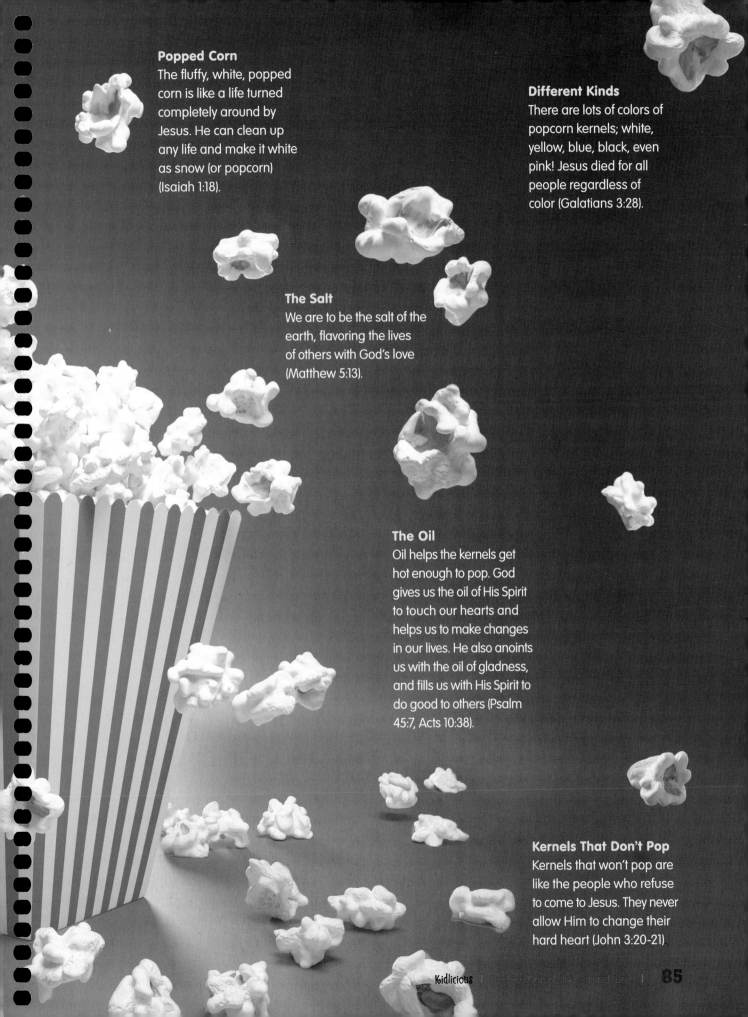

Popped Corn
The fluffy, white, popped corn is like a life turned completely around by Jesus. He can clean up any life and make it white as snow (or popcorn) (Isaiah 1:18).

Different Kinds
There are lots of colors of popcorn kernels; white, yellow, blue, black, even pink! Jesus died for all people regardless of color (Galatians 3:28).

The Salt
We are to be the salt of the earth, flavoring the lives of others with God's love (Matthew 5:13).

The Oil
Oil helps the kernels get hot enough to pop. God gives us the oil of His Spirit to touch our hearts and helps us to make changes in our lives. He also anoints us with the oil of gladness, and fills us with His Spirit to do good to others (Psalm 45:7, Acts 10:38).

Kernels That Don't Pop
Kernels that won't pop are like the people who refuse to come to Jesus. They never allow Him to change their hard heart (John 3:20-21).

Lunch
for
Teacher

Now that your lunches are the envy of the school, why not share your lunch making talents with someone? You can make a special lunch for your teacher on Teacher's Appreciation Day! Or maybe you can adopt a grandparent. Have Mom or Dad help you find an older person who doesn't cook much anymore, and take them a nice homemade lunch.

TOP SECRET

FOR PARENTS ONLY:

Going to school may seem like all fun and games for your kids, but it's really like going to work. There are good days and bad days. Your child may be feeling undue stress that he doesn't really know how to express. It helps them to feel better just knowing that you understand what they do all day. One great way to let kids know that you know what is going on in school is through their lunch box.

Maybe they are having a school spirit day where everyone has to wear red? Make a lunch with all red food. Are they studying Africa? Get recipes online or from a library book and pack an African lunch.

Maybe your child had an argument with a best friend yesterday. A simple little "I love you" note may bring cheer. Or perhaps a note to encourage him or her to say "sorry" is in order.

Just showing your kids that you know what is going on in their lives, and that you care about the things they do every day will create a bond and help them open up to you. When you know about all that is good and bad in their lives, you can help them learn how to make good decisions, and learn how to deal with life's problems.

MYSTERY IN THE CLASSROOM

CASE #4:

The Mysterious Instruction Book

Case Notes: Olivia's dad just got a new lawn mower. It came with an owner's manual that showed how to care for it, so it would run well and last a long time. Olivia thought about how nice it would be if our bodies came with an owner's manual. If people knew how to care for bodies, maybe they would not get sick as much and could live longer. Olivia decided to ask her pastor about her "owner's manual" idea.

 Watch for clues!

Interview Transcript:

Olivia: Pastor, did God really create me?

Pastor: Yes, He did. He created every one of us.

Olivia: If God created me, why didn't He give me an owner's manual so I will know how to take care of myself?

Pastor: He did! The Bible is your "Owner's Manual". It has a lot to say about how to take care of our bodies.

Olivia: It does? I had no idea! Does the Bible say which foods are best for our bodies?

Pastor: God said that He gave us plants, and all the fruit from trees to be food for us (Genesis 1:29). So, in the beginning, everyone was vegetarian, even the lions!

Evidence:
- God created us.
- God gave us a manual that helps us know how to take care of our bodies

THE VERDICT

We will test out the most of our foods that God showed them for us to eat.

The Family Meal

No broth on hand? Use
4 cups of water and 3
tablespoons chicken-style
seasoning

OH MY, POT PIE!

My friends at school loved this recipe...I think even the pickiest little brother would eat his veggies if they were covered with a kidlicious puppy face!

INGREDIENTS

- 2 tablespoons oil
- 1 cup onion, diced
- 4 stalks celery, diced
- 1 cup carrots, diced
- 1 teaspoon sage
- 1 teaspoon thyme
- 1 teaspoon marjoram
- 1 teaspoon salt
- 4 cups vegetable broth
- 4 medium potatoes, diced
- 1 cup green beans, fresh or frozen
- 2 cups non-dairy milk
- ¼ cup nutritional yeast flakes
- 3 tablespoons cornstarch
- 2 cups chicken substitute, diced (optional)
- 1 cup green peas
- 1 Pot Pie Crust (Page 106)

DIRECTIONS

1. Preheat oven to 400° and spray pie pans with non-stick cooking spray.

2. Heat oil in a large skillet over medium-high heat.

3. Add onion and cook until they begin to brown, about 7-8 minutes.

4. Add celery, carrots, sage, thyme, marjoram and salt. Cook for another 3-4 minutes.

5. Add potatoes, green beans and broth. Cook until vegetables are tender, about 15 minutes.

6. Mix yeast flakes and cornstarch with cold milk, and add to boiling vegetables. Stir until it thickens, about 1-2 minutes.

7. Stir in peas and chicken substitute, if using.

8. Pour into individual pie pans or a 9 x 13-inch baking dish.

9. Cover with crust or top with cute pie crust faces and bake for 20-30 minutes for the little pies or 30-40 minutes for a big pie, until crust is firm and edges are bubbly.

. . . .

 GLUTEN FREE Use a soy-based chicken substitute, or just leave it out. Leave off the crust, and serve with some crispy gluten free crackers.

Factories usually make foods with more fat and sugar than God intended (see Avoiding Food Fraud page 157).

INGREDIENTS

1 cup hot water

¼ cup chia seeds or flax seeds

1 box (14 ounce) water packed tofu, firm or extra firm, drained

1 box (12.3 ounce) silken tofu, firm or extra firm

3 cups TVP Beef Bits or other beef flavored TVP

2 cups small dry bread cubes (homemade or stuffing mix)

1 small onion, chopped

½ cup green pepper, chopped

½ cup soy cheese, shredded

3 tablespoons oil

1 tablespoon beef-like seasoning

1 teaspoon garlic powder

1 teaspoon salt

Topping

⅓ cup Real Tomato Ketchup (page 139)

¼ cup brown sugar

VEGGIE MEATLOAF

You can serve it as fun meatloaf cupcakes, or just make one big loaf like the rest of the world does. Either way you will want to save some leftovers of this for your lunch box! It's soooo good!

DIRECTIONS

1. Pre-heat oven to 325° and prepare muffin tins or 9 x 13-inch pan with non-stick cooking spray.

2. Mix hot water with chia seeds or flax seeds, and set aside.

3. Mix together topping ingredients, and set aside.

4. With clean hands, mix tofu, TVP, bread cubes, soy cheese, onion, green pepper, oil, beef seasoning, garlic powder, and salt together.

5. Add the chia seed mixture, and mix again.

6. For mini loaves, fill each muffin cup to the rim and press down firmly. For a larger loaf, form a loaf down the middle of a 9 x 13-inch pan, leaving room on both sides, and pressing together firmly.

7. Spread ¾ of the topping over the loaf or loaves. Cover and bake for 1 hour for the mini loaves or 1½ hours for the larger loaf.

8. Allow to cool about 30 minutes before removing from pan.

9. Spread with remaining topping. For mashed potato frosting, top with Mashed Potatoes (page 47).

LUNCH BOX: Meatloaf Sandwich (page 51). Need I say more?

GLUTEN FREE Use gluten free breadcrumbs.

Try This! Mashed sweet potatoes make a beautiful orange frosting.

Before people in the Bible started to eat meat, they lived for hundreds of years. After they started eating meat they lived much shorter lives.

STUFFED SHELLS

One of my favorites...it's really easy to make. I can almost make it all by myself!

INGREDIENTS

1 box jumbo shells

4 cups tomato sauce

1 recipe Tofu Ricotta (recipe below)

¼ cup non-dairy parmesan cheese (optional)

INGREDIENTS

2 packages (14 ounces) water-packed tofu, firm or extra-firm

1 package (8 ounces) frozen spinach, thawed and drained (optional)

1 cup soy sour cream

¼ cup lemon juice

¼ cup cane juice crystals or other sweetener

1¼ teaspoons salt

¾ teaspoon onion powder

¾ teaspoon garlic powder

DIRECTIONS

1. Preheat oven to 350°. Lightly coat a 9 x 13-inch baking dish with non-stick cooking spray.

2. Cook jumbo shells according to the package instructions.

3. Ladle 1½ cups of tomato sauce into the bottom of the pan.

4. Fill each shell with a spoonful of tofu ricotta and place in the pan on top of the sauce.

5. Cover with remaining sauce. Sprinkle with parmesan, if using.

6. Cover with aluminum foil, and bake 1 hour.

TOFU RICOTTA

1. Drain water from tofu and wrap tightly in 2 clean dry dishtowels and let sit for 20-30 minutes, to remove excess moisture.

2. In a large bowl, mash tofu with a potato masher or your hands.

3. Add remaining ingredients to tofu and mix well. Add additional salt or sweetener to taste.

Dinner Gift

Think of someone who just had a baby, or maybe someone who is in the hospital. I am sure the family would appreciate a nice home cooked meal. You could surprise them with this great dinner...after all, everybody loves pasta!

God made foods with the right balance of nutrients. Factories usually make foods with more fat and sugar than God intended (see Avoiding Food Fraud page 157)

BLACK BEAN SLIDERS

Miniature burgers are a fun way to change up the traditional burger and fries dinner. But don't forget to add some color with lettuce, tomato, onion, and maybe some avocado. These are "over the top good" with a nice pile of sweet potato fries!

INGREDIENTS

1 can (15 ounces) refried black beans or 2 cups cooked black beans, mashed

1½ cups quick oats

1 medium onion, diced fine

2 tablespoons vital wheat gluten flour

1½ tablespoons beef-like seasoning

1 tablespoon parsley

1 clove garlic, minced

DIRECTIONS

1. Pre-heat oven to 400° and prepare cookie sheet by spraying with non-stick cooking spray.

2. Mix all ingredients in a large bowl.

3. Form into patties, and place on oiled cookie sheet.

4. Cover with aluminum foil, and bake 20 minutes.

5. Remove cover, flip patties, and bake for 10 more minutes.

LUNCH BOX: Make a regular size burger for the Tex Mex Sandwich (page 51) in your lunch box.

I like to use a small ice cream scoop to make the patties all the same size.

MAC & CHEESE

You knew it was coming... every kid's cookbook has to have a macaroni and cheese recipe. Our Mac and Cheese is soooo creamy and cheesy you would never guess that it was dairy free! You can even make it gluten free, so everyone can have some!

INGREDIENTS

1 box (14 ounce) whole-grain or extra fiber pasta

1 cup cashew nuts

4 cups water, divided

1 cup shredded cheese substitute

¼ cup nutritional yeast flakes

1 tablespoon cornstarch

1 tablespoon lemon juice

2 teaspoons salt

1 teaspoon garlic powder

DIRECTIONS

1. Cook pasta according to the instructions on the box, drain and set aside.

2. Using a blender, blend cashews and 2 cups of water until very, very smooth, this will take several minutes.

3. Add the remaining ingredients except for the two cups of water, and blend again. Pour into a medium sized saucepan.

4. Add remaining 2 cups of water to blender and blend briefly, pour into pan with cashew mixture.

5. Cook over medium-high heat, stirring constantly until it comes to a boil and thickens.

6. Remove from heat, add pasta and stir together.

7. Serve as is, or place in a casserole dish and bake at 350° for 30 minutes.

If you need a nut free version of this recipe visit www.kidlicious.com because no kid should be without macaroni and cheese.

LUNCH BOX: Even just a little leftover Mac & Cheese makes a wonderful lunch treat. You can heat it in the morning and put it in your thermos or just eat it cold.

GLUTEN FREE Can be made gluten free with rice or quinoa noodles.

You could even use cookie cutters to cut fun shapes out of the dough.

God's whole plant food are good for your heart.

WONDER NUGGETS

Do you ever wonder what's in a chicken nugget? You don't have to wonder when you make your own! The best part is that your mom will be happy to serve these for dinner!

INGREDIENTS

1 package (14 ounce) water packed tofu, extra firm

1 can chickpeas, drained

¼ cup wheat germ or ground almonds

¼ cup flaxseed, ground

¼ cup nutritional yeast flakes

2 teaspoons poultry seasoning or chicken-style seasoning

1½ teaspoons onion powder

1 teaspoon garlic powder

1½ teaspoon salt

1 cup vital wheat gluten

½ cup water

2 tablespoons Braggs Liquid Aminos or low sodium soy sauce

Breading

1 cup non-dairy milk

2 cups cornflakes, crushed

DIRECTIONS

1. Drain water from tofu and wrap tightly in 2 clean dry dishtowels and let sit for 20-30 minutes, to remove excess moisture.

2. Preheat oven to 350° and line a large cookie sheet with parchment paper or spray with non-stick cooking spray.

3. Place the chickpeas, almond meal, flaxseed, nutritional yeast, poultry seasoning, onion powder, garlic powder and salt into the bowl of a food processor and pulse a few times until chickpeas are in small pieces.

4. Add tofu and pulse to combine all ingredients together. Add the vital wheat gluten and pulse until well mixed. Add wet ingredients and allow to process until a ball of dough is formed.

5. Place non-dairy milk and crushed cornflakes into separate shallow bowls.

6. Using a two-tablespoon scoop, make balls and flatten slightly into a nugget shape. Or you can roll out the dough about ¼ - ½ inch thick and cut into strips.

6. Dip each nugget or strip in milk then into the cornflake crumbs.

7. Place on a parchment lined cookie sheet. When sheet is full, cover with aluminum foil and bake covered for 25 minutes. Uncover and flip them over, and cook another 5-10 minutes until lightly browned and crunchy.

LUNCH BOX: Save a few nuggets for a Nugget Wrap (page 55) in your lunch box.

Whole plant foods help you to have more energy.

STROGANOFF

Grandma made Stroganoff all the time when she was growing up, and it was one of her favorites! Mom's version is a little healthier than Grandma's, so now she can eat more!

INGREDIENTS

1 tablespoon oil

1 medium onion, chopped

8 ounces fresh mushrooms, sliced

3 cloves garlic, minced

1 teaspoon thyme

½ teaspoon salt

¼ cup all purpose flour

3 cups Walnut Gluten (page 135) cut in strips, or vegetarian beef strips

1 cup raw cashews

3 cups water

DIRECTIONS

1. Heat oil in a large skillet over medium high heat.

2. Add onion and cook until it is translucent (almost clear), about 4-5 minutes.

3. Add mushrooms, garlic, thyme and salt, cook until water starts to come out of the mushrooms and they get a little brown.

4. While mushrooms are cooking, put flour in a plastic bag and add gluten strips. Toss together until strips are covered in flour.

5. Add flour-covered gluten strips to the cooked mushrooms, stirring occasionally.

6. Cook for another 5-8 minutes, until gluten strips are browned, stirring occasionally.

7. Using a blender, blend raw cashews with water until very, very smooth. This will take several minutes.

8. Pour cashew water mixture into the pan with mushroom mixture and stir together. Cook until mixture becomes thick. If the mixture gets too thick you can add a little water or milk to make a wonderful creamy gravy.

 LUNCH BOX: Just a little left over… perfect for your lunch!

 GLUTEN FREE Try this without the gluten and use more mushrooms. Leave out the flour but put 2 tablespoons of cornstarch in with the cashews and water to help it thicken.

You can cook 3 cups of dry beans and then use them in the chili instead of using canned beans.

God made lots of beautiful and colorful foods so He must want us to eat lots of colors.

GLUTEN FREE!

COLORFUL CHILI

Count them 1...2...3...4...5 colors in one pot of kidliciousness! Perfect!

INGREDIENTS

1½ teaspoons oil

1½ cups onions, diced

¼ cup green bell pepper, diced

3 cloves garlic, minced

1 package (12 ounce)
vegetarian burger

2 tablespoons chili powder

1½ teaspoons ground cumin

1 teaspoon paprika

½-1 teaspoon salt

¼ teaspoon oregano

¾ cup carrots, shredded

1½ cups corn, frozen or canned

2 cans (15 ounce) pinto beans,
drained and rinsed

1 can (15 ounce) red beans,
drained and rinsed

1 can (15 ounce) black beans,
drained and rinsed

2 cans (14 ounce) diced
tomatoes with green chilies

3½ cups water

DIRECTIONS

1. Heat oil in a large stockpot over medium heat.

2. Add onions, bell pepper and garlic, and sauté until the onions look translucent (almost clear), about 4-5 minutes.

3. Add vegetarian burger seasonings, and cook for another 2 minutes.

4. Add carrots, corn, beans, tomatoes and water, and bring to a boil.

5. Reduce heat and let simmer for at least 30 minutes, so all the flavors start working together.

LUNCH BOX: Cincinnati Chili is chili served over spaghetti noodles. Wouldn't you love that in your lunch box?

GLUTEN FREE Many people love all bean chili; just leave out the veggie burger. Or try a soy based TVP product to give a meaty texture.

Try This!

Roll out the left over piecrust and bake for about 10 minutes to make Pot Pie Crackers...very yummy with the pie!

POT PIE CRUST (OR CRACKERS!)

INGREDIENTS

2 cups whole wheat pastry flour (or one cup whole wheat flour and one cup unbleached white flour)

¼ cup nutritional yeast flakes

2 teaspoons paprika

1 teaspoon salt

1 teaspoon onion powder

⅛–¼ teaspoon cayenne (optional)

½ cup oil, chilled

½ cup water, very cold

DIRECTIONS

1. In a medium sized bowl, mix together flour, yeast flakes, salt, paprika, onion powder and cayenne.

2. In a separate bowl, mix together chilled oil and ½ cup very cold water.

3. Pour wet ingredients into dry ingredients and knead briefly to form dough.

4. Roll between two pieces of wax paper or plastic wrap.

5. Remove the top paper and gently flip dough onto Pot Pie (page 91) or use cutters and make into cute little puppy and kitty faces and bake as directed.

QUICK: Use 3 cups of frozen mixed vegetables instead of carrots, green beans and peas.

HUSH DOGGIES

Back in the old west, cowboys would toss little balls of corn bread to the dogs to keep them quiet at night. They called them hush puppies. We call these Hush Doggies because of the hot dogs inside.

INGREDIENTS

Dry Ingredients

1 cup whole wheat pastry flour (or ½ cup whole wheat flour and ½ cup white flour)

¾ cup corn meal

¼ cup cane juice crystals or sugar

1 tablespoon baking powder

1 tablespoon cornstarch

¾ teaspoon salt

Wet Ingredients

1 cup soy milk

2 tablespoons oil

5 vegetarian hotdogs, cut into 7 pieces each

DIRECTIONS

1. Preheat oven to 350° and prepare mini-muffin tins by spraying with non-stick cooking spray.

2. Mix the dry ingredients together in a medium bowl.

3. Add wet ingredients and stir together to make a thick batter.

4. Fill 36 mini-muffin tins about ¾ full with cornbread batter.

5. Add a slice of hot dog into each muffin. Don't try to cover them up, the batter will rise over the hot dog and make a cute dimple.

6. Bake for 20 - 25 minutes.

LUNCH BOX: Love these in the lunch box; it is just like a corndog…without the stick.

If you don't have mini muffin tins, you can make 8 large muffins and just add 4 slices of hotdog to each muffin. Bake 25 to 30 minutes.

Everybody in heaven is a vegetarian, so why not start early?!

TOFU SKILLET SUPER

I like this almost as much as pizza! Not that it tastes like pizza, but it is just its own kind of good. The tofu is my favorite part.

INGREDIENTS

2 packages (14 ounce) water packed tofu, extra firm

¼ cup Braggs Liquid Aminos or low sodium soy sauce

8-10 red skin potatoes, diced

2 teaspoons oil

1 small red onion, diced

1 small yellow or orange bell pepper, diced

1 teaspoon garlic, minced

1 bag (16 ounces) French cut green beans, frozen

1 teaspoon salt

1 teaspoon Italian seasoning

DIRECTIONS

1. Drain water from tofu, wrap tightly in 2 clean, dry dishtowels, and let sit for 20-30 minutes to remove excess moisture.

2. Cut tofu into one-inch cubes and place in a shallow dish. Pour Bragg's or soy sauce over the cubes. Allow the tofu to soak for about 10 minutes. This is called marinating.

3. While the tofu is marinating, boil or steam potatoes until a fork can be easily inserted into the potato.

4. Drain tofu and place in a large non-stick skillet over medium high heat. Cook, stirring occasionally until the tofu is lightly browned on all sides. Remove the cubes and set aside.

5. Add oil to the pan with onion, pepper, and garlic. Cook for 3-4 minutes.

6. Add potatoes, green beans, salt, and Italian seasoning. Cook for 10 minutes, stirring occasionally.

7. Stir in tofu and heat through.

MYSTERY IN THE CLASSROOM

CASE #5:

The Birthday Party Mystery

Case Notes: It's Dylan's birthday! His mom brought cupcakes, lemonade, and candy for the whole class. YEA!

About an hour after the party, it was hard for us to sit still and pay attention to the teacher.

Later that afternoon we all put our heads on our desks because we felt so tired.

Did something at the birthday party make us feel different?

 Watch for clues!

Evidence:

- The kids had a lot of sugar at the birthday celebration.
- After eating a lot of sugar it was hard to sit still and concentrate.
- Later on the kids were very tired.

THE VERDICT

There is nothing wrong with an occasional treat. But eating too much will make it hard to sit still and keep the energy small. It you do that, you will be able to sit still and pay attention in class. Besides that you'll feel terrific!!!

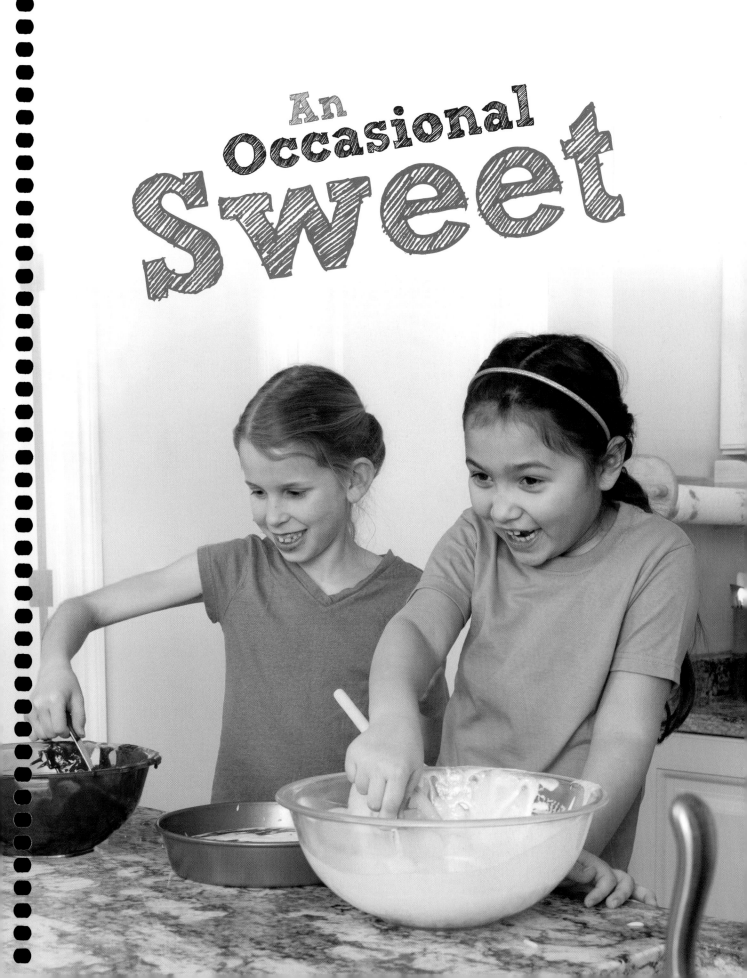

An Occasional Sweet

Zest is grated orange peel.
Use the smallest size grater
and just get the orange part.
Don't grate up the white
part because it tastes bitter.

Eating too much refined sugar makes it hard for your body to fight germs.

CUTIE PIE

One day we were eating an orange with the brand name "Cutie". All of a sudden my mom got excited. She said, "We have to make a 'Cutie Pie' for the cookbook!" So we practiced a little, and it turned out to be a brilliant idea.

INGREDIENTS

¼ cup raw cashews

½ cup cane juice crystals or sugar

½ cup orange juice

3 tablespoons cornstarch

2 teaspoons vanilla extract

1 package (12.3 ounce) silken tofu

Zest of one orange

Pinch of salt

2 cups clementine orange slices or 2 cans (11 ounces) mandarin oranges, drained and rinsed

6 graham crackers or crunchy cookies like ginger snaps.

DIRECTIONS

1. Blend cashews, cane juice crystals, orange juice and cornstarch until very smooth.

2. Pour into a pan and cook over medium heat until it becomes very thick. Stir this continually as it gets thicker to keep it from burning. You will end up with kind of a blob looking mixture.

3. Add this mixture to the food processor with tofu, vanilla, orange zest, and salt. Process until very smooth.

4. Add oranges and pulse until oranges are chopped.

5. Place graham crackers or cookies in the bottom of 6 individual serving dishes.

6. Pour pudding over cookies, cover with plastic wrap, and chill for at least 3-4 hours.

QUICK: If you absolutely can't wait to try your Cutie Pie you can eat it like a pudding.

 GLUTEN FREE Gluten free gingersnaps are easy to find and make a wonderful crust for these little cuties!

QUICK: Use baby food sweet potatoes or canned pumpkin.

Toast pecans by placing them on a cookie sheet in the oven while it pre-heats. By the time the oven is hot your pecans should be nicely toasted.

Look for added, refined sugar in all kinds of foods, even in places you don't expect it (learn how on page 157)

SUPERFOOD SURPRISE COOKIES

Mom, I need to eat more vegetables – can I have another cookie?!? That's right! The surprise in this cookie is a vegetable, but I promise you will never know. My daddy just couldn't believe Mommy when she told him! He asked her 3 times, and kept taking more cookies!

INGREDIENTS

¾ cup cane juice crystals or sugar

½ cup coconut oil or canola oil

¾ cup sweet potato, cooked and mashed

2 teaspoons vanilla extract

½ cup maple syrup or brown rice syrup

2½ cups whole-wheat pastry flour (or 1 ½ cups whole-wheat flour and 1 cup unbleached white flour)

1 tablespoon aluminum free baking powder

1 teaspoon salt

1½ cups toasted pecans, chopped

. . . .

Topping

¼ cup cane juice crystals

2 teaspoons cinnamon (optional)

DIRECTIONS

1. Preheat oven to 375°. Line a baking sheet with parchment paper or spray with non-stick cooking spray.

2. Mix topping ingredients together in a small bowl and set aside.

3. Use an electric mixer to combine oil with cane juice crystals. Mix in the mashed sweet potato, vanilla extract, and syrup until well combined.

4. In a smaller bowl, mix together flour, aluminum free baking powder, salt, and pecans. Add the dry ingredients to the wet ingredients and mix well.

5. Use a 2-tablespoon scoop to make a ball of dough. Place the ball in the topping mixture and roll until covered. Place on prepared baking sheet. Repeat until baking sheet is full.

6. Slightly flatten the cookies and bake for 13-15 minutes, until just starting to brown.

7. Remove from oven and let cool on the pan a few minutes, then place on wire rack to cool.

. . . .

Cookie Gift

Have you ever given much thought to the guy who picks up your trash? It must be hard work picking up trash all day. Let's surprise him with this fun little package. Make sure to put a big note on the package so he knows it is for him and not for the trash!

You can eat as much fruit as you want because the fiber will fill you up before you get too much sugar.

RICE CRISPY TREATS

Sweet. Chewy. Crunchy. Everything that a dessert should be! And I can share it with my gluten free friend at school!

INGREDIENTS

½ cup almond butter or peanut butter

½ cup maple syrup or brown rice syrup

¼ teaspoon agar powder (optional, but this really holds them together)

1 teaspoon vanilla extract

3½ cups crisp rice cereal

DIRECTIONS

1. Line an 8-inch square pan with parchment paper. This makes it easier to get the treats out of the pan later.

2. Heat nut butter, syrup and agar powder in a medium sized pan over medium high heat. Stir constantly until it begins to boil, then continue to stir for one minute before removing from heat.

3. Add vanilla and mix well.

4. Using a wooden spoon, stir in rice cereal until the cereal is completely coated with the mixture.

5. Pour mixture into the lined pan and press it down firmly so it will hold together.

6. Cut into 16 squares and allow to cool.

Rice Crispy Treat Gift

Our mail carrier does a great job delivering the mail every day, even in the rain and snow. I wonder if anyone remembers to say thank you? Wouldn't it be fun to say thank you with a treat in the mailbox! I bet it would make their day!

The best sweets to eat are natural sweets found in fruit. They contain natural sugar or "good" sugar along with fiber and vitamins.

CHUNKY MONKEY

GLUTEN FREE!

Love'n the Chunky Monkey! It is a three in one dessert that is perfect as a yummy crunchy chewy pudding treat. It also makes a great refrigerator cake (below). But if you freeze it, you have Chunky Monkey Fudgesicles (page 125). This stuff is just plain kidlicious!

INGREDIENTS

1 box (12 ounces) silken tofu

1 cup carob chips or non-dairy chocolate chips

2-4 tablespoons powdered sugar (optional)

1 teaspoon vanilla

3 bananas, diced

1 cup peanuts

½ cup coconut (optional)

½ cup raisins (optional)

DIRECTIONS

1. Place tofu and carob chips in a food processor and process until very smooth.

2. Add vanilla, and sugar if you are using it.

3. Pour tofu and carob chip mixture into a bowl.

4. Stir in diced bananas, peanuts, coconut and raisins.

5. Serve as a pudding or make into a Refrigerator Cake or Fudgesicles.

CHUNKY MONKEY REFRIGERATOR CAKE

A refrigerator cake is not really a cake at all. It is simply pudding with layers of cracker or cookies that you leave in the refrigerator overnight. I am thinking you might want to double this recipe... Just thinking...

INGREDIENTS

1 recipe Chunky Monkey (above)

11 whole grain graham crackers

DIRECTIONS

1. Place one layer of graham crackers in the bottom of a glass loaf pan.

2. Spread 1/3 of the Chunky Monkey Pudding over the crackers.

3. Place another layer of graham crackers over the pudding.

4. Spread 1/3 of the Chunky Monkey Pudding over the crackers.

5. Place another layer of graham crackers over the pudding.

6. Spread last 1/3 of the Chunky Monkey Pudding over the crackers.

7. Place in the refrigerator overnight, or at least for a couple of hours.

ZEBRA CAKE

Birthdays will never be the same again with this cool Zebra Cake. Who needs all that frosting when your cake has stripes?!? You are avoiding tons of fat and sugar, and impressing your friends all at the same time. How cool is that!?!

DIRECTIONS

1. Preheat oven to 350° and line 2 - 8 inch round cake pans with parchment paper. Just place each pan on the parchment and trace around the bottom with a pencil. Cut out the circle and fit it into the bottom of the pan. Spray with cooking spray.

2. Mix up Vanilla Cake and Carob Cake according to the directions to the right.

3. Using a ⅛ or ¼ cup measure, pour a scoop of the white mixture into the center, creating a small circle.

4. Using a different ⅛ or ¼ cup measure (use the same size as the one you used for the white mixture) pour a scoop of the dark mixture right into the center of the white mixture.

5. Keep alternating a scoop of each mixture until the pan is about half full. Repeat the process with the second pan.

6. If you're careful you should find concentric circles of alternating colors forming in the pan just like a big bulls eye.

7. Bake at 350° for 35-40 minutes.

Top with Coconut Whipped Topping (page 123)

Watch how it's done on **www.kidlicious.com**

INGREDIENTS

Dry Ingredients

1½ cups unbleached all-purpose flour

1 cup cane juice crystals or sugar

3 tablespoons roasted carob powder or cocoa powder

2 teaspoons aluminum free baking powder

½ teaspoon salt

. . . .

Wet Ingredients

⅓ cup oil

1 cup water

1 tablespoon lemon juice

1 teaspoon vanilla extract

CAROB OR CHOCOLATE CAKE

DIRECTIONS

1. In a large bowl, sift together flour, sugar, carob powder, baking powder and salt.

2. In a separate small bowl; mix oil, water, lemon juice and vanilla.

3. Add wet ingredients to dry ingredients and stir together, be careful not to over mix.

4. Bake according to directions for Zebra Cake.

You don't have to make a zebra cake. You can bake all of the batter in one 8-inch pan.

INGREDIENTS

Dry Ingredients

1⅔ cups all purpose unbleached flour

1 cup sugar

2 teaspoons aluminum free baking powder

½ teaspoon salt

. . . .

Wet Ingredients

1 cup water

⅓ cup oil

1½ teaspoons vanilla

VANILLA CAKE

DIRECTIONS

1. In a large bowl; sift together flour, sugar, baking powder and salt.

2. In a separate small bowl mix water, oil and vanilla.

3. Add wet ingredients to dry ingredients and stir together. Be careful not to over mix.

4. Bake according to directions for Zebra Cake.

LUNCH BOX: Add just a little to fresh or frozen fruit for a nice fruit salad dessert.

INGREDIENTS

¼ cup vanilla soy creamer or non-dairy milk

1 tablespoon maple syrup or other liquid sweetener (optional)

1 cup carob chips (barley malt sweetened), or non-dairy chocolate chips

You will probably need the extra maple syrup if you are using the non-dairy milk.

HOT FUDGE SAUCE

Perfect on fruit, ice cream (page 129), and even on oatmeal (page 7).

DIRECTIONS

1. In a small pan bring soy creamer and maple syrup to a boil.

2. Remove from heat, pour in carob chips, and stir until melted and very smooth.

3. If you are having trouble you can put the pan back on the burner for just a couple of seconds and keep stirring. Be extra careful because it burns easily.

INGREDIENTS

1 can (15 ounces) coconut milk

2-4 tablespoons powdered sugar or more to taste

1 teaspoon vanilla extract

Make ahead for Breakfast Banana Splits (page 7)

WHIPPED TOPPING

Light and fluffy, this is a beautiful topping for any dessert on earth!! Well almost any...

DIRECTIONS

1. Place the can of coconut milk and the metal bowl in refrigerator overnight.

2. Open the bottom of the coconut can and pour off the coconut water. What you have left is a firm layer of coconut cream.

3. Scoop out the cream into the chilled metal bowl.

4. Using your hand mixer whip the coconut cream for 3 to 5 minutes until it becomes fluffy and light, with soft peaks.

5. Mix in sugar and vanilla.

6. Use immediately, or keep for later. It stores well in refrigerator for several days.

It is better to eat fruit than to drink juice. When fruit is made into juice, it loses all its fiber.

FRUITSICLE

Way better than any fruit flavored popsicle you will find in the grocery store! I absolutely LOVE these!

INGREDIENTS

Fresh fruit (strawberries, kiwi, pineapple, peaches, whatever you like)

100% fruit juice (the lighter colored the juice the more you see the fruit)

INGREDIENTS

1 recipe Chunky Monkey (page 119)

Popsicle molds

DIRECTIONS

1. Cut the fruit in small pieces so that they can fit into the mold.

2. Stuff the Popsicle molds with fruit and pour juice over fruit to the fill line.

3. Place the Popsicle lid/sticks into the molds and place in the freezer.

4. Now this is the hard part. You have to wait until tomorrow.

5. Once the popsicles are frozen solid, take them out of the mold and enjoy.

CHUNKY MONKEY FUDGESCICLES

DIRECTIONS

1. Spoon Chunky Monkey pudding into popsicle molds.

2. Insert sticks and freeze overnight.

If you have trouble removing the popsicle, hold the cup end of the mold under hot water for a few seconds. The popsicle should slide right out.

Always eat your dessert with a high fiber meal. Fiber will slow down the sugar and give you long lasting energy.

FROSTY FRUIT

Fruits are an amazing summer treat. When frozen they become Kidlicious!

GLUTEN FREE!

INGREDIENTS

Grapes, washed

Cantaloupe, cut into bite size pieces

Honeydew, cut into bite sized pieces

Blueberries, washed and stemmed

Raspberries, washed

Bananas, peeled and cut into bite sized pieces

DIRECTIONS

1. Lay fruit out on cookie sheet in a single layer.

2. Place in freezer.

3. After 3-4 hours (or overnight) remove fruit from cookie sheet and place in a plastic container or zip top bag.

4. Store in freezer until you really need a cold treat!

Any time you have a little fruit left over, freeze it for the next hot summer day! Use leftover fruit from the Melon Kabobs (page 27)

When watching for refined sugar, you want to be careful of serving size. To learn more, see page 157.

FROZEN FRUIT ICE CREAM

Put this in an ice cream cone, a bowl or serve it up on a Gluten-Free Power Waffle (page 13) for a special breakfast! Your mom may protest a bit until she finds out it's fruit!

Banana Ice Cream

2 Bananas

Mixed Berry Banana Ice Cream

1 banana

½ cup frozen strawberries

½ cup frozen blueberries

Tropical Ice Cream

1 banana

½ cup frozen pineapple

¼ cup frozen mango

¼ cup toasted coconut

DIRECTIONS

1. Peel bananas, cut into 1-inch slices, place in a zip top freezer bag, and put in freezer overnight. The frozen bananas will keep in the freezer for several weeks.

2. Place frozen banana pieces in food processor. Pulse, then process until the bananas are the consistency of ice cream. It might take a few minutes, and you will have to scrape the sides and push down the bananas every once in a while.

3. Eat immediately, or place back in freezer to harden a little.

When your bananas start to get a few too many spots, slice them and store them in zip-top bags in the freezer to make some ice cream or maybe a Smoothie (page 131).

Try This!

Add 2 tablespoons of carob powder or chocolate powder at step 2.

When drinking juice or eating sugary foods, you can get a lot of calories and not even feel full.

LUNCH BOX: Pour leftover smoothie into a small lunchbox size container and freeze. Place in lunch box in the morning and by noon it will be thawed enough to call dessert!

GLUTEN FREE!

SMOOTHIES

If you haven't eaten enough colors today maybe you should have a smoothie. Smoothies really are the perfect food. They can be eaten for breakfast, lunch or supper, or even for dessert! Hmmm...I think I am going to go make a smoothie!

PB & J Smoothie

2 cups frozen banana chunks

1 cup frozen berries (whatever you like)

2 tablespoons peanut butter

1-2 cups 100% fruit juice of choice

Swamp Water Smoothie

1 cup frozen banana chunks

2 cups spinach

½ cup frozen pineapple chunks

1 orange peeled and seeded

½ cup frozen mango chunks

2 tablespoons fresh mint

1-2 cups apple juice

1 small piece fresh ginger, peeled (optional)

Breakfast Smoothie

1 cup silken tofu, drained

1 cup frozen strawberries

1 cup frozen banana chunks

1 cup orange juice

1 tablespoon flax or chia seeds

⅓ cup granola (optional)

The Usual Smoothie

2 cups frozen banana chunks

½ cup strawberries

½ cup blueberries

1-2 cups 100% apple raspberry juice

Neapolitan Smoothie

2 cups frozen banana chunks

1 cup strawberries

1-2 cups chocolate soymilk (more if needed)

1 teaspoon vanilla

Sunshine Smoothie

2 cups frozen Banana chunks

2 oranges peeled, no seeds

Zest of 2 oranges

1-2 cups orange juice

1 teaspoon vanilla

DIRECTIONS

1. Place all ingredients into blender and blend until smooth.

2. Add extra juice or milk if needed to keep the blender blades moving. The less juice or milk you add the thicker your smoothie will be.

Zest is grated orange peel. Use the smallest size grater and just get the orange part. Don't grate up the white part because it tastes bitter.

MYSTERY IN THE CLASSROOM

CASE #6:

Who Took My Cherries?

Case Notes: The kids in the classroom have been learning that you can't always judge a book by the cover. They were wondering if that was true of food packages too; so they each brought in a box, bottle, bag, or can and started to investigate.

 Watch for clues!

Interview Transcript:

Investigator: Alex, what did you bring?

Alex: I brought these cherry toaster pastries. They are organic, and natural, and there is a big picture of cherries on the box. I am sure they are healthy!

Investigator: Let's read the ingredients and see what is in them…flour, cane juice, oil, apples, flavoring… Hmmm, NO cherries at all!

Alex: How can they do that?! There is a picture of cherries right on the box! That's not fair! Someone stole my cherries!

Evidence:

• Many of the food boxes we checked looked better in the picture on the box than they did on the ingredient label.

• People who advertise foods are more interested in selling their product than in keeping you healthy. It is your job to read the label and choose foods that are best for you.

THE VERDICT one will steal your cherries!

know exactly what you are eating. That way no

Learn how to read a label on page 121 so you

Eat as many foods without labels as possible.

Eating Food
Without Labels....
Make it
Yourself!

Try This!
We use this in Stroganoff (page 103) but it works great as a meat substitute in a lot of recipes. Try it in your favorite stir-fry, or kebab, or whatever you like.

When buying food that has a label, don't look at the front of the box. Look at the ingredient list and the nutrition panel on the side (learn more about Avoiding Food Fraud on page 157).

WALNUT GLUTEN STEAKS

Gluten steaks are sometimes called wheat meat because they have a meat-like texture. But wheat meat, or gluten is actually made out of wheat. In the "olden" days, people had to make gluten from whole-wheat flour by washing it under water for a long time. Here's the new way to make gluten steaks from gluten flour.

INGREDIENTS

¼ cup walnuts

¼ cup quick oats

¼ cup nutritional yeast flakes

1 teaspoon salt

1 tablespoon onion powder

½ teaspoon garlic powder

2 cups water

2¼ cups vital wheat gluten flour

....

Broth

12 cups water

½ cup Bragg's® Liquid Aminos or low sodium soy sauce

1 teaspoon salt

1 tablespoon onion powder

1½ teaspoons garlic powder

¼ cup nutritional yeast flakes

½ teaspoon ground celery seed

1 tablespoon olive oil

1 teaspoon basil

DIRECTIONS

1. Blend walnuts, quick oats, yeast flakes, salt, onion powder, garlic powder and water until smooth.

2. Place gluten flour into a large mixing bowl and pour in contents of blender.

3. Mix well, knead with hands for 1-2 minutes.

4. Shape into 2 logs, wrap in plastic wrap, and refrigerate for 2 hours or overnight.

5. The next day, mix all broth ingredients together in a large pan and bring to a boil.

6. Slice gluten logs into ¼ inch slices and carefully drop into boiling broth.

7. Reduce heat and simmer for about 1 hour.

....

Watch us make this on **www.kidlicious.com**.

Pickle Gift

A jar of homemade pickles makes a perfect gift to show appreciation to someone. Next time you drive by the fire department, why not use a jar of homemade pickles to show them that you are glad they are always there to help the community!?!

If you don't have jars, mix in a glass bowl. Just make sure the cucumbers are under the brine (water and lemon mixture).

If you make your own food from scratch there is no label, and you know exactly what is in it.

GLUTEN FREE!

INGREDIENTS

- 1 cup lemon juice
- 1 cup water
- 1 cup honey or other sugar
- ½ teaspoon celery seed
- ½ teaspoon turmeric
- 2 pinches cayenne pepper (optional)
- 3 tablespoons canning or kosher salt
- 4 bell pepper slices
- 4 onion slices
- 8 cups cucumbers, sliced

BREAD & BUTTER REFRIGERATOR PICKLES

Here is a shocking fact...pickles are cucumbers. Who would have known!

DIRECTIONS

1. Place lemon juice, water, honey, celery seed, turmeric, cayenne and salt in a medium sized saucepan. Cook over medium heat until the salt and honey dissolve.

2. Place 2 slices of onions and 2 slices bell pepper in the bottom of 2 wide-mouth canning jars and fill with as many sliced cucumbers as you can fit in each jar.

3. Carefully pour the liquid mixture in the jars, completely covering the cucumbers.

4. Put the lids on and refrigerate for at least 24 hours.

INGREDIENTS

- 2 cups water
- 1 cup lemon juice
- ¼ cup canning or kosher salt
- 2 cloves garlic
- 2 onion slices, thick
- 2 tablespoons dill weed or dill seed
- 8 cups cucumber, thinly sliced

LEMON DILL REFRIGERATOR PICKLES

These are so easy to make and so much more kidlicious than those from the store! You will wonder why you never made your own in the first place!

DIRECTIONS

1. Mix water, lemon juice, and salt together.

2. Place 1 clove of garlic, 1 slice of onion and 1 tablespoon of dill seed in 2 wide-mouth canning jars. Fill with as many cucumbers as you can fit in the jar.

3. Carefully pour the liquid mixture into the jars, completely covering the cucumbers.

4. Put the lids on and refrigerate for at least 24 hours.

Regular table salt works okay too, it will just make the liquid cloudy.

God doesn't label the food He makes because you can count on Him to make it just the way it should be. Check out the produce department for some great foods without labels.

GLUTEN FREE!

REAL TOMATO KETCHUP

Did you know that most ketchup has more sugar per cup than ice cream! Who wants all that sugar when you can easily make your own ketchup from real tomatoes! You'll love this version because it tastes nice and fresh. If you want more of a traditional flavor you can add 1/3 cup of white vinegar.

INGREDIENTS

6 cups fresh tomatoes, diced

½ medium onion

3 cloves garlic

¼-½ cup cane juice crystals or sugar

⅔ cup lemon juice

1 tablespoon salt

DIRECTIONS

1. Place all ingredients into a large saucepan and bring to a boil over medium high heat.

2. Cook until mixture reduces by at least one half, about 30-45 minutes. Just keep cooking until half of the tomato mixture has boiled away. Then allow to cool slightly.

3. Place contents of pan into blender and blend until smooth.

4. The ketchup will thicken more as it cools, but if you would like it a little thicker you can mix in a couple of tablespoons of tomato paste.

Don't Forget to Share

Very few people have ever had homemade ketchup from real tomatoes, so anyone would be excited to receive this as a gift. After all who doesn't like ketchup?

Read your labels to make sure you are getting the kind of food that will help you grow strong and healthy.

Check out www.Kidlicious.com for a "how to" video on bread making and more ideas of what you can do with that dough.

OATMEAL BREAD

There is nothing like homemade bread. It smells so good and tastes even better! It takes some time to make, but it's a bit like playing with play dough, so it doesn't seem like long at all!

INGREDIENTS

3 cups water

1 cup rolled or quick oats

¼ cup oil

½ cup honey, cane juice crystals, or other sweetener

½ tablespoon salt

½ tablespoon lecithin granules

5-6 cups whole wheat flour

½ cup gluten flour

1½ tablespoons instant active dry yeast

DIRECTIONS

1. Place water and oats in a bowl and allow to soak for 20-30 minutes. Or you could use leftover oatmeal from breakfast. If using leftover oatmeal, mix together 1 cup of precooked oatmeal and two cups of warm water.

2. Measure all ingredients, except 2 cups of the flour, into the bowl of a mixer that has a dough attachment. Start mixer on the lowest speed and allow to mix for 1 - 2 minutes.

3. Gradually add in the additional flour as needed until the dough pulls away from the bottom and sides of the bowl. The dough should be soft and a bit sticky. Allow to knead for 7 minutes.

4. Preheat oven to 350° and prepare pans by spraying with non-stick cooking spray.

5. Put a little flour on your counter top to keep the dough from sticking. Place dough on floured counter top and divide into 3 equal portions. Make each lump of dough into a ball and allow to rest on the counter for 15 minutes.

6. Shape dough into loaves or make Scripture Surprise Bread as a gift (see below) or Pizza Rolls (page 67). Put in pans. Cover the loaves with a damp or slightly wet dishtowel and let sit on the counter until dough doubles in size, 45 minutes to 1 hour.

7. Bake 35-40 minutes, remove from oven and place on cooling rack until cooled.

Try This!

Add 1½ cups of raisins and 1 teaspoon of cinnamon near the end of the kneading process. If you add them too early your raisins will fall apart.

Scripture Surprise Gift

You can hide a Scripture verse inside the bread by wrapping it in aluminum foil or parchment paper and placing it inside the loaf before you shape it. Then when they cut the bread they get a surprise. We like to hide Bible promises in our bread.

CASE #7:

Mystery of Levi's Sleepless Nights

Case Notes: Levi is tired all the time. The strange thing is that he can't get to sleep at night. Why can't he sleep when he is so tired?

 Watch for clues!

Interview Transcript:

Investigator: What do you like do in your spare time?

Levi: I like to play computer games. I don't have much energy, so usually I watch TV or play with my games.

Investigator: Do you ever go outside and play?

Levi: I only play outside at school recess, but I don't have fun. I am too tired to run a lot.

Evidence:

- Levi does not exercise.
- Levi feels tired.
- Levi can't sleep at night.

THE VERDICT

It will spend up more a day working hard or playing active games, he will be able to sleep at night and will have more energy all day.

All Together Now...

SPONGE BALLS

Hot summer day? Does dad have you out working in the yard? Hard work like mowing, raking, and planting flowers is great exercise. When the work is all done, why not get the family into a sponge ball fight? These sponge balls are really quick and easy to make, and perfect for a hot day. Keep a bucket of cold (maybe a little ice) water around to dip them in, and then take aim!

To Make a Sponge Ball:

To make a sponge ball, cut 2 rectangular sponges into 3 equal strips. Use dental floss or fishing line to tie them together in the middle. Be sure to tie your lines very tightly. Twist the sponge pieces around to form a ball!

KICK THE CAN

Have you ever-played Kick the Can? It is an old game, but a fun one for the whole family to play. You will need at least three players, a can, room to run, and places to hide.

Rules of the Game:

One player is chosen to be "It." The can is placed in an open space. "It" stands by the can and counts to 30 while the other players hide. Once "It" is finished counting, he or she tries to find and tag the other players. Once a player is tagged, he or she is out until the next round. Any player who has not been caught can kick the can, and if this is done without the player being caught first, he or she wins the game. If "It" tags every player, then "It" wins the game. If you have very young players, they can be on a "team" with someone else and work together. Remember this is all for fun. Everyone should take turns being "It". If someone is having a hard time, help them out by working as a team.

SNOW!

- Don't be afraid of a little cold. When was the last time your mom built a snowman?

- Going sledding is a fun activity for kids of all ages.

- Make a fort, if you live in one of those places that gets a lot of snow. You can make snow bricks by packing a small wastebasket or bucket with snow. Dump it out and you have a brick! Do it lots of times for lots of bricks, and you have the coolest snow fort ever.

BALLOON PING PONG

Clear the dining room table and play a fun game of Balloon Ping Pong. Make balloon ping pong paddles by taping craft sticks or paint stirring sticks to paper plates. Use your dining room table as your playing surface. Inflate balloon and start having fun!

HOT & COLD

You only need two people to play this game but you can always have more. Select a small item that can be hidden, like a small stuffed animal. Send all of the players out of the room while one person hides the item. Once the item is hidden, invite everyone back in to find the hidden item.

If someone gets close to the item, tell them that they are hot. If someone is far away, let them know they are cold. You can tell them when they are getting warmer or getting colder. When they get really close, tell them they are burning hot and almost ready to catch fire. If you want to make the game fun for a small child, hide a phone or something else that makes a noise. Let them follow the sound to find the hidden treasure.

STATUES IN THE PARK

This is a fun and active game that is the opposite of musical chairs. In this game, everyone has to jump and wiggle around and act silly until the music stops. Once the music stops everyone freezes like a statue. The "park ranger" then walks through the statues to make sure none of the statues are moving. Whoever gets caught moving has to sit down until everyone else gets caught.

INDOOR SNOWBALL FIGHT

Is it too cold for your little sister to go outside? Or maybe there is no snow in your town? No problem! Have an indoor snowball fight! Pairs of socks make great snowballs.

How to Play:
Divide the family into teams, clear out a little space, use the couch as a shield, and start throwing "snowballs". You can end the evening with some popcorn and hot cocoa, just like you would after a real snowball fight. The biggest problem will be figuring out whose socks are whose when it's all over.

WHEELBARROW

Divide into teams of two. It's okay to have only one team. One partner holds the second partner's ankles in the air as the second partner walks forward on his or her hands to see how far they can go. If you have a couple of teams you can race.

Be a Blessing to Someone

Create a Blessing Jar and fill it with little notes about fun things your family can do for others. Pick out one note each week and do the good deed. Here are a few ideas to get you thinking.

➡ **Visit** someone who is in the hospital.

➡ **Adopt** a grandparent at a local nursing home.

➡ **Babysit** for a single mom.

➡ **Cook** some food for your local fire department.

➡ **Go** to the park and pick up trash before you play.

➡ **Welcome** a new family to the neighborhood with a Nacho Ordinary Neighbor gift .

➡ **Read** about a missionary, then pray for him or her, and send a care package. See **www.afmonline.org** for some great stories.

➡ **Do** yard work for an elderly neighbor.

➡ **Make** cookies and a thank you note and leave them in the mailbox for your mail carrier.

➡ **Take** a meal to a new family.

Suggestions for Reading...

➡ Read or study the Bible.

➡ Read a true mission story telling how God worked miracles in people's lives.

➡ Read a biography of a famous person who did great things for others.

➡ Read about scientific inventions, and the people who discovered them.

At the End of the Day

After all the fun, you will want to end family night (or every night) with a special family bonding time.

Let each person share the best thing that happened that day. Talk about how God gives His blessings. Let each person tell about the worst part of the day. Talk about how trials help us to be stronger, and how we can handle those hard times better in the future. Read a worthwhile book together. It doesn't matter how old the kids are. There is something good about hearing dad or mom's voice, and sharing the experience of the story. It can strengthen family relationships. Reading together enriches the family as a whole.

You can adjust the story to the age of your children, but don't be afraid to read something the young kids won't completely understand. You will be surprised at what they do get, and listening will increase their vocabulary and their desire to read on their own. Of course they don't have to sit and do nothing! Let them color and listen at the same time. Suggest that they illustrate a favorite part of the story.

MYSTERY
IN THE CLASSROOM

CASE #8:

The Secret
Happy Medicine

Case Notes: Lily had a terrible day! Everything went wrong! All she wants to do is sit around and complain about it. How can we help her get out of this bad mood?

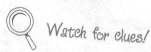 Watch for clues!

Interview Transcript:

Lily: First, my alarm clock didn't go off, and I slept in too late. I missed breakfast AND the bus. When I got to school I saw that the teacher was unhappy because I missed....

Investigator: Wait! Wait! Stop! Talking about all your troubles is going to make you feel worse. Have you ever heard the proverb that says a happy heart does good like a medicine?

Lily: I would love a happy heart, but I don't have one! I have a sad heart.

Investigator: Well I know where you can get a happy heart! If you do something nice for someone you will feel a lot happier!

Lily: What can I do?

Evidence:
- Talking about our problems makes us feel worse.
- Giving gifts is a fun way for us to share happiness with others.

THE VERDICT

Making an effort to be kind to others, even when we don't feel like it, can make us both happy and healthy.

Better to Give Than to Receive

- Neighbors

- Teacher

- Elderly people

- Librarian

- Doctor

- A friend from church

- Sanitation Engineer (the guy who picks up the trash)

- Fireman

- Policeman

- Mail delivery person

- Someone in the hospital

- Someone just out of the hospital

- Someone with a new baby

- Someone having a bad day

- The checkout person at the grocery store

GIFT INDEX

Johnny Appleseed is known for spreading apple seeds all over the United States. Maybe you can become a legend too, by spreading smiles all over your town. You will be amazed at how much fun you can have delivering delicious goodies that you made yourself! When you spend your time on being kind to others, you will find you have less time to worry about your own problems. You are guaranteed to be happier!

Spread a Little Love

Family Fun Gift Basket

Share your family fun with someone else. Do you know a family that doesn't get much family time? Maybe they just don't know what to do! Take some time on your family night to build a basket of family fun for a family you know.

Blessing Jar

Decorate a cute jar. Fill it with family night ideas that you think the family will enjoy. Spend one of your family nights brainstorming ideas and creating the jar. You'll be creating special memories for yourselves, and you'll feel great about being a blessing to others.

Winter Outdoor Basket

Sometimes the hardest time to find something to do is in the winter. Why not give someone a Snowman Building Kit? Include a scarf, hat, carrot, and big buttons for eyes. Don't forget to include some hot cocoa mix and one of your favorite missionary stories so they can read together when they come in from the cold.

Winter Indoor Basket

Instead of giving cookies as a gift, give them the ingredients to make their own! Include the recipe, and instructions to wrap some of them up and give them to someone they know.

Game Night

Many families like to have movie night together, but movies don't encourage family togetherness. It's way more fun when everyone is laughing and talking together about real life stuff. Instead of a movie night basket give your friends a popcorn gift basket and add a fun game that your family enjoys.

AVOIDING FOOD FRAUD

Do you like to decipher secret codes? The only way to know for sure that you are not the victim of food fraud, and to know exactly what you are eating, is to learn the code on the Nutrition Facts Label. It is not hard to figure out. There are just a few things you need to know. The best place to start is at the top.

THE SERVING SIZE is the key to the whole puzzle. A serving is the amount of the food they think you will eat. If they think you should eat a ½ cup serving, but you really eat a whole cup, then all the other numbers on the label should be twice as big. For example, a bottle of soda may look like just enough for you to drink, but the label may say it has 2 servings. If the label says a serving has 10 grams of sugar, but you drink the whole bottle (2 servings) then you have just had 20 grams of sugar.

CALORIES are energy. You may think that more energy is better, but that is not exactly how it works. We only burn up a certain number of calories a day while growing, working and playing. If you eat more calories than you burn up, they become fat. That puts you at risk for health problems. Not all calories are the same. Calories that come from fats can be a problem for your heart. You don't want to eat too many of them.

You don't have to worry too much about calories if you follow the Portion Plate Rule (page 159) when you eat healthy meals with your family. But if you snack a lot, or eat out of packages instead of made-from-scratch family meals, add up those calories to make sure you don't get too many.

PROTEIN is important because it is the building block for our cells. It helps our muscles to grow strong. God put plenty of protein in plant-based foods such as vegetables, grains, beans and nuts. As long as you eat a good balanced diet and follow the Portion Plate Rule (page 159) you won't have any problems.

Nutrition Facts

Serving Size: 1 bar (2.1 oz/59g)
Serving Per Container: 1

Amount Per Serving

Calories: 249   Cal from Fat: 112

% Daily Value*

Total Fat 12g	**19%**
Saturated Fat 1.7g	**8%**
Trans Fat 0g	**0%**
Cholesterol 0mg	**0%**
Sodium 19mg	**1%**
Total Carb 31g	**10%**
Sugars 16g	
Dietary Fiber 5g	**20%**
Protein 8g	

Vitamin A 1% • Vitamin C 1%

Calcium 4% • Iron 7%

*Percent Daily Values are based on a 2,000 calorie diet

FAT: We all need some fat in our foods to keep us healthy. Healthy fats can be found in plant foods like olives, nuts and even avocados. Avoid foods with cholesterol and trans fats because they are hard on your heart. You will want the saturated fat number to be very low, or even 0. These bad kinds of fats are usually in foods that come from animals or that have been processed in a way that makes them clog up your heart.

SUGARS: We all know what sugar is, and we know it tastes good! But too much makes it hard for our bodies to stay healthy. This part of the label is the trickiest part! It includes added sugar AND natural sugar! The natural sugar is good for us and comes from foods God made for us. The refined sugar is man-made. You need to read the ingredient label on page 158 to decipher this code. If the food has raisins or other fruit near the beginning of the ingredient list, the sugar number will be higher because of the natural fruit. But if it lists sugar first, or has 3 different kinds of sugar, you know it's got way too much of the wrong kind of sugar.

FIBER: We learned a lot about fiber in the Lunch Box section starting on page 48. Fiber helps you feel full, and it acts like a scrub brush to clean out your intestines. It is always good to keep things clean! What would happen if you never cleaned out your closet? Look for whole-grain foods that have at least 3g of fiber per serving. Remember that the serving size thing works with good things, too. If ½ cup of cereal has 3 grams of fiber and you eat a whole cup, you have 6 grams of fiber…good for you!

VITAMINS AND MINERALS These are the things that help keep your body working. It's good to have numbers higher than 20% if you can, but most foods are high in some things and lower in others. That is why it is important to eat a variety of different foods to get a good balance of all of the vitamins and minerals you need.

Vitamin A 1% • Vitamin C 1%

Calcium 4% • Iron 7%

*Percent Daily Values are based on a 2,000 calorie diet.

INGREDIENTS: Water, Honey, Soy Sauce, Brown Sugar, Vinegar, Soybean Oil, Rice Vinegar (Water, Rice, Sugar Cane, Sugar, Salt), Roasted Garlic concentrate (Roasted Garlic, Dextros, Salt, Canola Oil, Garlic Powder, Water, Modified Food Starch, Autolyzed Yeast Extract, Citric Acid, Natural Flavoring) Tomato Paste (Tomato Paste, Salt, Citric Acid), Mustard Powder, Maple Syrup, Citric Acid, Spices, Guar Gum, Xanthan Gum, Caramel Color.

INGREDIENT LABEL:

The package ingredient label lists the item that has the largest quantity first. The second ingredient is a smaller amount, clear down to the last item of which there is the smallest amount. If you are buying an apple pie you would hope the first ingredient would be apples, right?!? If the first item is sugar, you might want to eat something else.

Another thing to check on the ingredient label is the length of the list. The longer the ingredient list, the farther it is from the way God made it. It is a good thing if you recognize all of the ingredients. Food names that you understand let you know that there is some natural food that God meant for you to eat. If the food is full of chemicals you cannot pronounce, it is likely a counterfeit someone invented to trick you into eating something that is not good for you.

PORTION PLATE RULE

When you fill your dinner plate, think of dividing it into three parts.

- Fill one whole side of your plate with fruits and vegetables.

- Now divide the other side of your plate in half. Fill half of the half with whole grains like breads, cereals, brown rice, or starchy vegetables like potatoes, corn, or squash.

- The last piece of your plate should have something high in protein like beans, tofu, nuts, or meat substitutes.

It should look something like this.

Just Remember This

#1 Check Servings — are you actually eating 1, 2, or 3 servings?

#2 The numbers in red should be lower: fat, cholesterol, sodium, sugar.

#3 The numbers in green should be higher: fiber, protein, vitamins.

#4 Check the ingredient list: Is it long or short? Is the first ingredient a good one?

Now you have to decide if this is the right food for you!

FOR PARENTS ONLY:

Just one thing!

If there was one thing that you could do to help your children stand up to peer pressure and make better choices, would you do it? If that "one thing" was proven to help your children choose better friends and get better grades in school, would you do it?

What if that same thing had also been shown by research to improve family relationships so dramatically that your teens would rather confide in you with serious problems instead of peers? Lastly, what if this "one thing" will also help your children and teens make better food choices so that they would be less likely to become obese and less likely to develop eating disorders? Does it sound too good to be true?

The researchers from The National Center on Addiction and Substance Abuse (CASA) at Columbia University released a study showing that the simple act of eating dinner together just five times a week would do all of that, and more.

Now that you know what that "one thing" is, will you do it? To some it may seem like an impossibility to get the whole family together for a meal one day a week, let alone five! But as you can see, it is well worth the effort.

Now don't be thinking that the first time your whole family sits around a table together it's going to be like a Norman Rockwell painting,

Eating 1 sit-down meal a day, five days a week will make your kids...

42% less likely to drink

50% less likely to smoke

66% Less likely to smoke marijuana

Less likely to get into fights and be promiscuous

More likely to get A's & B's in school

with everybody living happily ever after! It may feel strained and awkward at first. After all, it may be something entirely new to everyone! You may even get some push-back from the kids, but keep working at it. I can guarantee one thing: If you persist in keeping up a positive conversation and attitude, it will all be worth it in the end. One day the kids will all move out. When you and hubby are eating alone, I can promise that you will never say, "I wish we had not taken all that time and energy to eat with the kids when we could have been watching TV!"

But the actual cooking of those meals — who is going to do that? The whole family of course! When kids help to create their own food, they are more likely to eat it. That means more happy faces at the dinner table! As a side benefit, they also learn self-reliance, creativity, teamwork, preferring others above themselves, and even how to stay within a budget. When kids cook with their parents, they have more quality family time. They gain a sense of belonging, and of being a part of something good.

So let's get that whole family in the kitchen and turn it into the place where the family gathers to share stories and real life experiences. It's much better than gathering in the living room and sharing the lives of imaginary people on TV shows.

Now you know the secret "one thing" that can bring maximum benefit to your family. Are you willing to do it? Make your home a little slice of heaven on earth. The next time you sit down for a family meal, give thanks to God who gives you the blessing of good food and also the blessing of a family united.

In a recent Time Magazine article by Nancy Gibbs it was revealed that the more often families eat together, the less likely they are to smoke, drink, do drugs, get depressed, develop eating disorders, and consider suicide. Children that eat with their families regularly are more likely to do well in school, delay having sex, and make healthier food choices. "It teaches vocabulary, and how to have a conversation and solve problems. It is about teaching them to be a part of their culture."

10 WAYS TO GET YOUR KIDS TO EAT REAL FOOD

1. Have them help you cook the food. Yes, they will make a mess, but it gives you an opportunity to teach them how to clean it up. Life skills learned are more important than the mess! Be sure to affirm their efforts, so they'll want to keep trying!

2. Let them be creative. Have them pick out a new fruit or veggie at the store and try it. Let them pick a recipe from the cookbook to try.

3. Eat together as a family. No kids menu, no TV, no phone. If you are serving something new or something you know your child has not "learned to like," serve other foods you know they will eat along with the new food.

4. You don't have to like it. You just have to taste it. Research shows that a child (or adult) needs to taste something 10 - 15 times before they accept it as a food. If they taste it and don't like it, that is okay. They are learning to like it. Serve it regularly and have them taste it again and again. Taste buds do change.

5. Eating together is fun! Make mealtime the most enjoyable time. Don't rush and hurry! Talk together and get to know each other. Get the kids in on the conversation. Let them know that this is their time to share. It will be hard at first but your patience will be rewarded.

6. Be positive about food. Don't make dinner a struggle. Never get into a battle of the wills with your child. If they win once, it will be that much harder the next time. Don't count bites or make them eat. They won't starve to death if they don't eat. Hunger is sometimes the best seasoning.

7. No snacking. This is a throw-back to the good ole days of not spoiling your dinner. Kids need to realize that it is okay to feel hungry between meals. They are less likely to eat a good meal if they know a more appealing snack is coming in a couple hours.

8. Don't use food as a bribe or reward, or even just to keep from being bored. This could set up the dangerous habit of emotional eating as they become adults.

9. Eat mostly real, plant-based foods, prepared at home. Think colorful fruits and vegetables, whole grains, nuts, and beans.

10. Don't sabotage the taste buds with too many refined foods. Occasional treats or "unhealthy" foods are fine just as long as they don't become part of the regular diet. Birthday cake is great on your birthday, but not so great every day of the week. And watch out for those "flavor blasters" like the chips and crackers with an extra "burst" of flavor. No natural food will ever match up to those overly processed tastes. Real food tastes best when taste buds aren't corrupted by overly refined foods or artificial "flavor blasters".

GLOSSARY

Aluminum-free baking powder: A dry white powder that creates bubbles in a batter to make light and fluffy baked goods. It is used in cookies, cakes and muffins. Some baking powders contain aluminum, which is not good for our bodies. We use either the Featherweight brand or the Rumford brand. Both are available at any health food store.

Beef style seasoning: A popular all-purpose seasoning used in vegetarian cooking to give a "beefy" type flavor. We use Vegetarian Express brand in our recipes (thevegetarianexpress.com).

Bragg's Liquid Aminos: A non-fermented soy sauce that is lower in sodium (salt). We like it because it has a lighter taste. You can find it at your health food store, or just use light soy sauce from the grocery store.

Cane juice crystals: This is also called raw sugar or turbinado sugar. It is just sugar that is in a more natural form than the highly refined sugars most often used. It is darker in color than regular table sugar because some minerals remain. Almost all of these are usually removed during the processing which makes the sugar white. Use cane juice crystals cup-for-cup to replace white sugar in any recipe. You can buy this at most grocery stores in the sugar section.

Carob: Also called St. John's bread, carob is believed by many to be the food that John the Baptist ate in the wilderness. It comes from the locust bean pod. Carob adds flavor and vitamins to desserts. Many people use it as a chocolate substitute because it contains important vitamins that chocolate does not have. Unlike chocolate, carob does not contain any caffeine, which can be harmful to our bodies. Carob is available in powder form (similar to cocoa powder) and candy form (similar to chocolate chips). We recommend the barley sweetened carob chips, which do not contain partially-hydrogenated oils. Look for carob at the health food store.

Chia Seeds: Full of omega-3 fatty acids and antioxidants, chia seeds are extra good for you. The good news is, they taste great! Actually, they don't have much of a taste. But that is good because we can add them to all sorts of things without changing the flavor of our food. We get the health benefits without spoiling our favorite dishes. Chia seeds can be used as an egg replacer similar to flax seeds. Chia seeds have the advantage that you don't have to grind them, and they don't go rancid as quickly. Just add 1 tablespoon of chia seeds to 3 tablespoons of hot water. Let sit for 10-20 minutes, and you'll have a substitute for one egg. We use chia seeds in the Meatloaf (page 93) and in our Refrigerator Oatmeal (page 21).

Chicken style seasoning: This is the most popular all-purpose seasoning in the vegetarian world. It is great in a lot of recipes, and some people even eat it on popcorn. Our favorite brand is from The Vegetarian Express. We also use McKay's Chicken Style seasoning. Be sure to look for the dairy-free and MSG-free version. You will need to buy this at your health food store.

Chicken substitutes: These include any homemade or store-bought soy or wheat products used to replace chicken in recipes. There are many options. You can find them on the internet by looking for lightlife.com, morningstarfams.com, yvesveggie.com, tofurky.com, or gardein.com. Many of these are available in the produce department next to the tofu, or in the frozen food section of your grocery store.

Flax seeds: These small brown seeds are slightly larger than a sesame seed. Flax seeds are full of nutrients including omega-3 fatty acids, calcium, iron, niacin, and vitamin E. The seeds are most easily absorbed when ground. When mixed with water, they become viscous (gooey like an egg white), adding moisture and binding qualities to your baked goods without the cholesterol of eggs. To replace one egg just add 1 tablespoon of ground flax seeds and 3 tablespoons of hot water, and let sit for a minute or two before using. Once flax seeds are ground, store them in the freezer to keep them from going rancid. Look for flax seeds in the baking isle of your grocery store.

Garbanzo flour: It is simply ground up garbanzo beans. Garbanzo flour is really good for you because it is high in protein and fiber. You can find it in most grocery stores in the gluten free baking section, or in the international section of the store. If you have a high power blender, you can make your own by putting dry garbanzo beans in the blender and blending them to a powder.

Gluten flour: Another name for gluten flour is vital wheat gluten. It is a part of the wheat kernel that is almost entirely protein. It is used in making meat substitutes like our Walnut Gluten (page 135) Do not confuse this with "high-gluten flour" which is used for baking bread. You can buy vital wheat gluten in the baking isle of your grocery store.

Natural peanut butter: Simple and pure, the only ingredients in natural peanut butter are peanuts and sometimes salt. Because there is no partially hydrogenated oil in natural peanut butter, the oils separate. Stir the oil in before use. Store the peanut butter in the refrigerator after you stir it to keep it from separating again.

Non-dairy milks: There are many good options, including soy, rice, almond, oat, and hemp milks. Most are fortified with calcium, vitamin D, and vitamin B12. Some contain sweeteners and flavorings such as vanilla, chocolate, and carob. Taste and richness varies from brand to brand, so keep trying different options until you find the one you love.

Non-hydrogenated margarine: There are no dairy products or trans-fats in these great substitutes for butter or regular margarine. Use them in baking and cooking just as you would use butter. There are many brands available. Earth Balance and Smart Balance Light are the brands that we use most often because they are available at the grocery store.

Nondairy cheese: Substitutes for dairy cheese come in several varieties, such as slices, shreds, and blocks. Many flavors are available such as cheddar, American, pepper-jack, and Parmesan. Some of these cheeses are very good and others are not. Try different ones to find your favorite. Our favorite brand is made by Galaxy Nutritional Foods because it is most affordable and easy to find at a health food store. It's even in some grocery stores.

Nutritional yeast flakes: Here is an easy and tasty way to get a lot of B vitamins, including B12. Those who don't eat meat or dairy need a good source of B12. Nutritional yeast has a unique cheesy type flavor that we use in a lot of recipes. Find it at your local health food store.

Pickles or pickle relish: We love to use pickles cured in lemon juice instead of the traditional pickles cured in vinegar. Vinegar can cause some stomach and digestion problems. Lemon juice, on the other hand, is good for you. It helps you to absorb more vitamins. Besides, the taste of the lemon juice pickles is 100% better. You can find the good kind of pickles at the health food store or make your own (page 137). Pa's brand is our favorite (pasfoods.com).

Raw cashews: Cashew nuts that have not been roasted or salted give a nice creamy texture to sauces when blended with water until smooth. They are a great source of protein and antioxidants. Look in the produce department of your grocery store for a variety of raw nuts.

Soy curls: This is a meat substitute produced by Butler. It is made from the whole soy bean that has been lightly textured. Soy Curls come dry and require "re-hydration". They also require quite a lot of seasoning to give them the desired flavor. We use it in "B" (page 59), for the BLAT Wrap, and BLT Pasta Salad. Soy Curls can be used as a chicken substitute in many recipes. They are especially good for those who need to eat gluten free (butlerfoods.com).

Soy cream cheese: When you need a dairy-free cream cheese that has a smooth creamy texture, there are several excellent choices. Soy cream cheese can be used interchangeably in recipes calling for cream cheese. We like to use Tofutti Cream Cheese, which is non-hydrogenated (tofutti.com).

Soy mayonnaise: A mayonnaise made without eggs is naturally cholesterol-free. Our favorite brand is Vegenaise for its rich taste and creamy texture (followyourheart.com). But new varieties are becoming available over time.

Soy sour cream: Tofutti "Better than Sour Cream" is our favorite commercial sour cream substitute made from soy. It contains no hydrogenated oils, cholesterol, or dairy (tofutti.com). You can find it at the health food store. Some grocery stores carry it in the natural food section.

Tofu: The "curd" made from soy milk is much like cottage cheese which is made from cow's milk. Tofu comes in two major forms. The water-packed variety requires refrigeration and has a shelf life of about 1 month. This type can be used as a meat, egg, or even cheese substitute. The silken variety is shelf stable for up to 6 months and is very smooth. It is best used in creams and sauces that are blended.

TVP: Textured Vegetable Protein is usually made from soybeans that have been processed to have a texture similar to meat. It comes dry, and has to be reconstituted with water or other liquid to make it look and taste good. It is available at health food stores.

Vegenaise: This is the name brand of the most widely available soy mayonnaise. Although it is cholesterol free, it is still very high in fat. It is one of those foods that is good if you don't eat too much of it.

Vegetarian burger: Affectionately called "veggieburger", this wheat or soy based product looks and tastes like ground beef. It works as a great low fat, cholesterol free substitute in many recipes that call for ground meat. It is available at many grocery stores in the produce isle near the tofu. If you can't find it in your grocery store, it will be available in a health food store.

Vegetarian lunchmeat: A variety of wheat or soy based products are designed to look and taste like your favorite meat slices. The slices come in flavors like bologna and turkey. Many grocery stores carry vegetarian lunchmeat in the produce isle near the tofu. If you can't find it in your grocery store it will be available in a health food store. Our favorite brands are Tofurky, Lightlife Deli Slices, and Yves.

Whole-wheat flour: This flour is made from hard winter wheat berries with a high gluten content, which makes it perfect for bread. It is made from the entire wheat berry, unlike white or unbleached flour, so it retains all of the vitamins and nutrients found in wheat.

Whole wheat pastry flour: When making cakes and cookies, it's best to use a flour made from soft spring wheat berries with a low gluten content. We like to use white whole-wheat flour if we can find it, because it is made from the entire wheat berry and is full of vital nutrients. It is lighter in color and makes our cookies and cakes come out lighter and fluffier. You can also use a combination of whole-wheat flour and unbleached white flour as a replacement for whole-wheat pastry flour.

Yogurt: Many non-dairy yogurts are available to replace dairy yogurt. Soy is the most common but you can find almond and coconut milk yogurts as well. It comes in many flavors and can be used in recipes for baking, topping a fruit salad, or just eating plain! Be sure to check the ingredients, because some soy yogurts contain dairy. Our favorite brands are Silk and Stonyfield Farm.

INDEX

RECIPE NOTES

RECIPE NOTES